Shortcuts to 100 Best Latin Recipes

Shortcuts to 100 Best Latin Recipes

Authentic Flavors Without the Trouble

Sergio E. Yibrin

iUniverse, Inc.
New York   Lincoln   Shanghai

Shortcuts to 100 Best Latin Recipes
Authentic Flavors Without the Trouble

iUniverse books may be ordered through booksellers or by contacting:

iUniverse
2021 Pine Lake Road, Suite 100
Lincoln, NE 68512
www.iuniverse.com
1-800-Authors (1-800-288-4677)

Because of the dynamic nature of the Internet, any Web addresses or links contained in this book may have changed since publication and may no longer be valid.

The views expressed in this work are solely those of the author and do not necessarily reflect the views of the publisher, and the publisher hereby disclaims any responsibility for them.

Illustrations copyright © 2007 SYZ Properties, LLC, employer-for-hire of Monique Rodrigue

ISBN: 978-0-595-46827-0 (pbk)
ISBN: 978-0-595-91117-2 (ebk)

Printed in the United States of America

To my parents:
Lutfy Yibrin and Jeanette Zarhi de Yibrin

Contents

Acknowledgments

Thank you to everyone who helped with ideas, taste testing, feedback, and endless support while I was creating the recipes for the book you are holding in your hands today.

I would also like to thank Monique Rodrigue for making my recipes come alive on the pages through her beautiful illustrations.

Finally, I want to thank iUniverse for its support through the entire production process, from editing my manuscript to the final publication.

Introduction

The ever-growing popularity of Latin American cuisine—noticed through the steady increase of Hispanic products in large supermarkets and new Latino restaurants throughout the United States—and today's fast-paced lifestyle gave birth to this book, *Shortcuts to 100 Best Latin Recipes: Authentic Flavors Without the Trouble.*

Traditionally in Latin American countries, many people still cook their meals from scratch; however, to achieve delicious, fast, and simple Latin favorites, I combined convenience foods such as canned beans, pre-minced garlic, pre-shredded coleslaw mix, and store-bought broth, among others, with fresh ingredients to make easy, homemade-tasting meals.

This book was a lot of fun to put together; it took a lot of imagination and time to create all these delicious recipes I am glad to share with you.

Drinks
Bebidas

Drinks/Bebidas

Banana Milk Shake
Batido de Banana

As a Honduran, I just couldn't leave this recipe out of this book. Bananas are one of Honduras' main agricultural products. This batido makes an excellent breakfast substitute rich in potassium.

2 ripe bananas (see "tip")
4 cups milk
$\frac{1}{4}$ cup sugar, or to taste
Pinch of ground cinnamon

1. Place all ingredients in a blender. Cover and blend on low speed about 1 minute, or until smooth. Pour into 4 or 6 tall glasses. Serve immediately.

Yield: 4 to 6 Servings

Tip:

✓ Ripe bananas should have a bright yellow skin with small, brown flecks. However, if you are unable to find ripe bananas, buy green or semi-ripe bananas (bananas with a yellow skin and a little green on the ends and along the ridges) and let them ripen at room temperature on your kitchen counter.

Banana
Milk Shake

Blackberry Juice
Jugo de Mora

Fruit juice is a popular drink choice in Latin American menus. Jugo de mora is among the most popular ones. Deep red in color and sweet and tart in taste, it offers a colorful and healthy alternative to soft drinks due to its antioxidant benefits.

4 cups water
$^1/_3$ cup sugar, or to taste
1 (16-ounce) bag frozen blackberries

1. Bring water to a boil in a medium saucepan over high heat. Remove from heat. Add sugar and blackberries; stir until sugar dissolves. Let cool 15 minutes.
2. Transfer blackberries and water to a blender. Cover and blend on low speed about 1 minute, or until smooth. (Depending on blender size, you might have to blend the juice in two or more batches.) Strain into a pitcher. Cover and refrigerate about 2 hours, or until thoroughly chilled. Discard blackberry seeds. Stir before serving.

Yield: 4 to 6 Servings

Corn Drink
Atol de Elote

Atol de elote, original to El Salvador, is enjoyed throughout Central America. As bizarre as it may sound, this exotic, thick, rich drink is simply delicious.

4 cups milk, divided
2 tablespoons cornstarch
1 (1-pound) bag frozen yellow whole kernel corn, thawed
1 cup sugar
Pinch of ground cinnamon

1. Place $1^1/_2$ cups of the milk, cornstarch, corn, sugar, and cinnamon in a blender. Cover and blend on low speed about 2 minutes, or until smooth. Strain into a medium nonstick saucepan. (Stir and press corn pulp against strainer with back of a large spoon to help liquid pass through.) Add remaining $2^1/_2$ cups milk; stir well. Discard corn pulp. Cook over medium heat, stirring continuously, 18 to 20 minutes, or until slightly thicker. (see "tip") Remove from heat. Let cool.
2. Transfer drink to a pitcher. Cover and refrigerate about 4 hours, or until thoroughly chilled. Stir before serving.

Yield: 4 to 6 Servings

Tip:

✓ Because this drink scorches easily, it is very important to use a nonstick saucepan and to stir continuously through cooking. However, if it does scorch, don't panic, and do not scrape burnt drink off the saucepan. Personally, I like it when it scorches a little bit. It gives the drink a very distinctive and pleasantly smoky flavor.

Piña Colada

"Piña colada" literally translates to "strained pineapple" in English. This tropical drink originated in Puerto Rico and has become extremely popular throughout the world. Some like it to taste more like pineapple rather than coconut and vice versa, while others prefer more rum, less rum, or no rum at all (virgin). The ingredient ratios are personal preference. This is the way I like mine.

$1^{1}/_{2}$ **cups pineapple nectar**
$^{1}/_{4}$ **cup coconut cream**
$^{1}/_{4}$ **cup dark rum (optional)**
4 cups ice cubes
4 maraschino cherries, for garnish

1. Place pineapple nectar, coconut cream, rum (if using), and ice in a blender. Cover and blend on high speed about 1 minute, or until smooth. Pour into 4 tall glasses. Garnish each with 1 cherry. Serve immediately.

Yield: 4 Servings

Rum and Cola
Cuba Libre

Ironically, this Latin favorite called "Cuba libre" literally translates to "free Cuba" in English. Some refer to it as "la mentirita", which means "the small lie". Salud!

Ice cubes
2 ounces dark rum
4 lime wedges
Diet or regular cola

1. Fill 4 tall glasses with ice. Pour $^1/_2$-ounce rum into each glass. Squeeze and drop 1 lime wedge into each glass. Fill each glass with cola; stir well. Serve immediately.

Yield: 4 Servings

Tamarind Slush
Hielo de Tamarindo

Tamarind is a very popular fruit throughout the Caribbean and Central America. It has a pleasantly tart—yet, sweet—taste. You can find canned tamarind nectar in Latin or Asian markets and large supermarkets.

4 cups ice cubes
2 cups tamarind nectar
1 teaspoon lime juice

1. Place all ingredients in a blender. Cover and blend on high speed about 1 minute, or until slushy. Pour into 4 tall glasses. Serve immediately.

Yield: 4 Servings

Appetizers

Aperitivos

Appetizers/Aperitivos

Bite-Size Guacamole Tostadas
Tostaditas de Guacamole

These are the miniature version of the famous Mexican tostadas. Store-bought tortilla chips speed up the assembling process.

48 store-bought bite-size round tortilla chips
1 cup "Guacamole" (see page 17)

1. Arrange tortilla chips on a large platter. Top each with 1 teaspoon guacamole. Serve immediately.

Yield: 48 Tostaditas

Cheese Quesadillas
Quesadillas de Queso

A Mexican favorite! Quesadillas can be prepared with numerous fillings; however, cheese is the only ingredient that must remain the same in all the different recipes. It is the binder that keeps all components together. I like to keep mine easy, simple, and cheesy.

4 (8-inch) soft taco-size flour tortillas, divided
2 cups finely shredded Mexican cheese blend
Store-bought salsa

1. Heat a nonstick griddle (comal) over medium heat.
2. Place 2 of the tortillas on a work surface. Sprinkle each with 1 cup cheese. Top each with remaining 2 tortillas.
3. Cook quesadillas on griddle about 1 minute per side, or until cheese is melted and tortilla is crisp and light brown. Let stand 1 minute. Cut each into 8 wedges. Serve with salsa immediately.

Yield: 4 Servings

Chilean Avocado Cream
Crema de Palta

A party favorite! The recipe for this delectable dip comes from my Chilean mother, Jeanette Zarhi de Yibrin. Serve it with store-bought plantain, tortilla, or yucca chips. It will be a hit.

2 large ripe Hass avocados (see "tip")
$1/_4$ cup cilantro leaves
$1/_4$ cup chopped yellow onion
$1/_2$ teaspoon store-bought minced garlic
2 tablespoons olive oil
2 tablespoons lime juice
1 teaspoon salt
Pinch of ground cayenne pepper
Pinch of ground cumin

1. Cut avocados in half, lengthwise. Remove and discard pits; scoop out flesh into a food processor. Add cilantro, onion, garlic, oil, lime juice, salt, pepper, and cumin; cover and process about 1 minute, or until smooth. Transfer to a medium glass or plastic bowl. Cover and refrigerate 1 hour before serving.

Yield: About $1^1/_2$ Cups

Tip:

✓ Ripe avocados should yield to the touch but still be firm. If you are unable to find ripe avocados, buy unripe avocados and let them ripen at room temperature on your kitchen counter.

Chilean Baked Turnovers
Empanadas de Horno Chilenas

A staple in the Chilean cuisine! I cannot imagine a Chilean home or restaurant without these empanadas. The various recipes are slightly different; however, most are similar. Using frozen dough disks for turnover pastries (discos de masa congelados para empanadas), found in the frozen section of Latin markets or large supermarkets, makes this recipe very easy.

1 (10-count) package frozen dough disks for turnover pastries, thawed
1¹/₄ cups "Chilean-Style Ground Beef" (see page 48), drained and cooled
10 pitted black olives
2 hard-boiled eggs, peeled and sliced
1 (1.5-ounce) box raisins

1. Heat oven to 350º F.
2. Place 1 dough disk on a work surface. Spoon 2 tablespoons meat on center; top with 1 olive, 1 or 2 egg slices, and a couple of raisins. Brush edge with water. Fold in half to form a half-moon. Seal edge by crimping with a fork. Place empanada on an ungreased baking sheet. Repeat with remaining dough disks.
3. Prick a few holes in empanada tops with a fork.
4. Coat empanada tops with cooking spray.
5. Bake empanadas 15 to 18 minutes, or until light brown. Serve immediately.

Yield: 10 Empanadas

Conch Ceviche
Ceviche de Caracol

Ceviche is extremely popular throughout the Caribbean and Latin America. It is a mixture of raw fresh fish or shellfish, citrus juice, vegetables, and spices. The seafood is cooked by the acid in the citrus juice after marinating for a couple of hours. This ceviche is made with conch, a popular shellfish in the Caribbean and Central America, which can be found in Latin or Asian markets and specialty seafood stores. This is how my Honduran aunt, Mayra Alvarenga de Yibrin, makes hers. Serve it with crackers or store-bought plantain chips.

1 pound conch, cleaned and chopped
1 cup lime juice
3 cups chopped tomato
$^1/_2$ cup finely chopped green bell pepper
$^1/_4$ cup finely chopped red onion
$^1/_4$ cup cilantro leaves, coarsely chopped
1 teaspoon store-bought minced garlic
$^1/_2$ cup ketchup
1 tablespoon olive oil
$^1/_2$ teaspoon salt
$^1/_4$ teaspoon ground cayenne pepper
$^1/_4$ teaspoon ground cumin
Pinch of sugar

1. Combine conch and lime juice in a medium glass or plastic bowl; mix well. Cover and refrigerate overnight.
2. Drain conch, reserving $^1/_4$ cup lime juice.
3. Transfer conch to a clean medium glass or plastic bowl. Add reserved $^1/_4$ cup lime juice, tomato, bell pepper, onion, cilantro, garlic, ketchup, oil, salt, pepper, cumin, and sugar; mix well. Cover and refrigerate 1 hour; stir before serving.

Yield: About 5 Cups

Cuban Picadillo Turnovers
Empanadas con Picadillo Cubano

A Cuban favorite! As with "Chilean Baked Turnovers" (page 14), using frozen dough disks for turnover pastries (discos de masa congelados para empanadas), found in the frozen section of Latin markets or large supermarkets, makes this recipe extremely easy.

Vegetable oil, for frying empanadas
1 (10-count) package frozen dough disks for turnover pastries, thawed
$1^{1}/_{4}$ cups "Cuban-Style Ground Beef" (see page 51), drained and cooled
Salt and ground black pepper

1. Pour oil into a large skillet to a depth of 1-inch; heat over medium heat.
2. Meanwhile, assemble empanadas. Place 1 dough disk on a work surface. Spoon 2 tablespoons meat on center. Brush edge with water. Fold in half to form a half-moon. Seal edge by crimping with a fork. Place empanada on an ungreased baking sheet. Repeat with remaining dough disks.
3. Fry empanadas in batches, about 2 minutes per side, or until golden brown. Drain on paper towels. Sprinkle with salt and pepper. Serve immediately.

Yield: 10 Empanadas

Guacamole

Viva Mexico! We need to thank Mexicans for this wonderful avocado dip. It's a must-serve for any occasion. Serve it with tortilla chips.

2 large ripe Hass avocados (see "tip")
2 tablespoons lime juice
$^1/_2$ teaspoon salt
Pinch of ground cayenne pepper
2 tablespoons finely chopped red onion
$^1/_2$ cup finely chopped tomato
$^1/_4$ cup cilantro leaves, chopped
$^1/_2$ teaspoon store-bought minced garlic
1 jalapeño pepper, seeded and finely chopped

1. Cut avocados in half, lengthwise. Remove and discard pits; scoop out flesh into a medium glass or plastic bowl. Add lime juice, salt, and pepper; mash with a fork to a chunky paste. Add onion, tomato, cilantro, garlic, and pepper; gently mix well. Cover and refrigerate 1 hour before serving.

Yield: About 2 Cups

Tip:

✓ See tip on page 13.

Honduran Molten Beans
Fundido de Frijoles

"Fundido", which literally translates to "molten" in English, is referring to the melted cheese within the beans; thus, explaining how this dish got its name. Traditionally, it's served in clay bowls that sit over charcoal to keep the beans warm and the cheese melted. However, due to clay bowls limited availability, I call for a ceramic fondue pot, which can be found in most kitchen accessory stores, to prepare this dish. I like to think of it as a beans-and-cheese fondue.

2 cups "Refried Beans" (see page 90), heated
1 cup shredded mozzarella cheese
Store-bought tortilla chips

1. Combine beans and cheese in a medium microwave-safe dish; mix well. Microwave on high about 2 minutes, or until cheese is melted; mix well. Transfer to a pre-greased warm ceramic fondue pot. Serve with tortilla chips immediately.

Yield: 4 Servings

Mini Honduran-Style Enchiladas
Enchiladitas Hondureñas

This is the bite-size version of the "Honduran-Style Enchiladas" (page 54). Because of their similarity, I like to serve them at the same time I serve "Bite-Size Guacamole Tostadas" (page 11) to offer colorful one-bite nibblers.

48 store-bought bite-size round tortilla chips
1 heaping cup "Refried Beans" (see page 90)
Grated Parmesan cheese

1. Arrange tortilla chips on an ungreased baking sheet. Top each with 1 teaspoon beans.
2. Heat oven to 350º F.
3. Bake enchiladitas 5 minutes, or until thoroughly heated. Sprinkle each with cheese. Serve immediately.

Yield: 48 Enchiladitas

Salsa Fiesta with Plantain and Tortilla Chips
Fiesta de Salsas con Tajaditas de Plátano y Totopos

The different salsas called for in this recipe offer several flavors and textures. It's a great choice to add color and fun to the table for get-togethers.

1 cup "Avocado and Mango Salsa" (see page 33)
1 cup "Central American-Style Salsa" (see page 34)
1 cup "Chilean-Style Salsa" (see page 35)
1 cup "Pico de Gallo" (see page 36)
Store-bought plantain and tortilla chips

1. Spoon each salsa into individual serving bowls. Serve with plantain and tortilla chips.

Yield: 4 to 8 Servings

Soups

Sopas

Soups/Sopas

Cuban-Style Black Bean Soup
Sopa de Frijoles Negros Estilo Cubano

Black bean soup is extremely popular throughout Latin America. The different versions among each country are endless. I chose to share the Cuban version.

1 tablespoon olive oil
$^1/_2$ cup chopped yellow onion
$^1/_4$ cup chopped green bell pepper
$^1/_4$ cup chopped celery
$^1/_4$ teaspoon ground cumin
$^1/_8$ teaspoon ground cayenne pepper
1 tablespoon store-bought minced garlic
1 (15-ounce) can black beans, undrained
2 cups store-bought low-sodium chicken broth
1 bay leaf

1. Heat oil in a medium saucepan over medium heat. Add onion, bell pepper, celery, cumin, and pepper; cook and stir about 5 minutes, or until vegetables are softened. Add garlic; cook and stir 30 seconds. Add beans, broth, and bay leaf; stir well. Bring to a boil. Reduce heat to low. Simmer, stirring occasionally, 10 minutes.
2. Remove saucepan from heat. Discard bay leaf. Puree soup with a hand-held immersion blender on low speed. Serve immediately.

Yield: 4 Servings

Honduran-Style Conch Soup
Sopa de Caracol Estilo Hondureño

This thick and chunky soup best resembles New England-style chowder. The different ways to prepare it are many. This particular recipe comes from my Honduran aunt Mary Canahuati de Yibrin. Serve it with a side of "White Rice" (page 96).

1 tablespoon "Annatto Oil" (see page 117) or canola oil
$^1/_2$ cup chopped yellow onion
$^1/_4$ cup chopped green bell pepper
$^1/_4$ cup chopped celery
$^1/_2$ teaspoon salt
$^1/_2$ teaspoon ground cayenne pepper
$^1/_4$ teaspoon ground cumin
1 tablespoon store-bought minced garlic
1 tablespoon masa harina
1 cup diced mirliton
1 cup diced carrot
1 cup diced yucca
1 cup diced green banana (see tip)
4 cups store-bought low-sodium chicken broth
1 (13.5-ounce) can coconut milk
1 bay leaf
1 pound conch, cleaned and cut into 1-inch cubes
1 tablespoon chopped cilantro leaves

1. Heat oil in a large saucepan over medium heat. Add onion, bell pepper, celery, salt, pepper, and cumin; cook and stir about 5 minutes, or until vegetables are softened. Add garlic and masa harina; cook and stir 30 seconds. Add mirliton, carrot, yucca, banana, broth, coconut milk, and bay leaf; stir well. Bring to a boil. Cook, stirring occasionally, 5 minutes.
2. Add conch and cilantro; stir well. Cook, stirring occasionally, about 5 minutes, or until vegetables are tender. Discard bay leaf. Serve immediately.

Yield: 6 Servings

Tip:

✓ To peel a green banana, cut off both ends, crosswise; score skin several times, lengthwise; peel skin away.

Pork Crackling Soup
Sopa de Chicharron

Pork cracklings are a Latin American favorite. They give this soup its exceptional flavor. This particular recipe comes from my Honduran friend and caterer Waldina Fernandez. Serve it with a side of "Cilantro Rice" (page 78).

1 tablespoon "Annatto Oil" (see page 117) or canola oil
$^1/_2$ cup chopped yellow onion
$^1/_4$ cup chopped green bell pepper
$^1/_4$ cup chopped celery
$^1/_4$ teaspoon salt
$^1/_8$ teaspoon ground cayenne pepper
$^1/_8$ teaspoon ground cumin
1 tablespoon store-bought minced garlic
6 cups store-bought low-sodium chicken broth, divided
1 (4-ounce) bag pork cracklings (see "tip")
1 green plantain, peeled (see "tip") and cut crosswise into $^1/_2$-inch-thick pieces
$^1/_2$ pound sweet potatoes, peeled and cut into $^1/_2$-inch pieces
1 (6-count) bag frozen half-ears of corn-on-the-cob, thawed
1 bay leaf
$^1/_4$ cup cilantro leaves

1. Heat oil in a large saucepan over medium heat. Add onion, bell pepper, celery, salt, pepper, and cumin; cook and stir about 5 minutes, or until vegetables are softened. Add garlic; cook and stir 30 seconds. Add 1 cup of the broth and pork cracklings; stir well. Bring to a boil. Remove from heat. Let stand 5 minutes.
2. Transfer pork crackling mixture to a food processor. Cover and process about 1 minute, or until pureed. Pour back into saucepan. Add remaining 5 cups broth, plantain, potatoes, corn, and bay leaf; stir well. Bring to a boil over medium heat. Reduce heat to low. Cook, stirring occasionally, about 13 minutes, or until vegetables are tender.
3. Add cilantro; stir well. Discard bay leaf. Serve immediately.

Yield: 4 to 6 Servings

Tip:
- ✓ Sometimes it's easier to find 4-ounce pork crackling bags in convenience stores at gas stations than in supermarkets because of their snack size.
- ✓ To peel a green plantain, cut off both ends, crosswise; score skin several times, lengthwise; peel skin away.

South American-Style Chicken Soup
Sancocho de Gallina

Popular in Colombia and Venezuela, this soup has crossed borders throughout South America. Traditionally, it is made with "gallina" which literally translates to "hen" in English. I prefer to prepare mine with chicken.

1 tablespoon canola oil
$^1/_2$ cup chopped yellow onion
$^1/_4$ cup chopped green bell pepper
$^1/_4$ cup chopped celery
$^1/_2$ teaspoon salt
$^1/_4$ teaspoon ground cayenne pepper
1 tablespoon store-bought minced garlic
12 cups store-bought low-sodium chicken broth
1 (4-pound) store-bought whole cut-up chicken, skinned and rinsed
1 bay leaf
$^1/_2$ pound sweet potatoes, peeled and cut into $^1/_2$-inch pieces
$^1/_2$ pound yucca, peeled and cut into 1-inch pieces
1 (6- or 8-count) bag frozen half-ears of corn-on-the-cob, thawed
1 green plantain, peeled (see "tip") and cut crosswise into $^1/_4$-inch-thick pieces
2 tablespoons chopped cilantro leaves

1. Heat oil in a large saucepan over medium heat. Add onion, bell pepper, celery, salt, and pepper; cook and stir about 5 minutes, or until vegetables are softened. Add garlic; cook and stir 30 seconds. Add broth, chicken, and bay leaf; stir well. Bring to a boil. Cook, stirring occasionally, 25 minutes.
2. Add potatoes, yucca, corn, and plantain; stir well. Return to a boil. Cook, stirring occasionally, about 10 minutes, or until vegetables are tender.
3. Add cilantro; stir well. Discard bay leaf. Serve immediately.

Yield: 6 to 8 Servings

Tip:
    ✓   See tip on page 25.

Tortilla Soup
Sopa de Tortilla

A Mexican classic! The different versions are endless. Mine uses masa harina (corn masa), the flour used to make corn tortillas in Latin America, to give it an intense tortilla flavor. Masa harina can be found in Latin markets or large supermarkets.

Soup:
2 tablespoons "Annatto Oil" (see page 117) or canola oil
$^1/_2$ cup chopped yellow onion
$^1/_4$ cup chopped green bell pepper
$^1/_4$ cup chopped celery
$^1/_2$ teaspoon salt
$^1/_4$ teaspoon ground cumin
$^1/_8$ teaspoon ground cayenne pepper
1 tablespoon store-bought minced garlic
$^1/_4$ cup masa harina
5 cups store-bought low-sodium chicken broth
1 bay leaf
1 tablespoon chopped cilantro leaves

Garnish:
Vegetable oil, for frying tortilla strips
8 (6-inch) white corn tortillas, cut into thin strips
1 large ripe Hass avocado (see "tip"), pitted, peeled, and chopped
Store-bought pepper jack cheese cubes

1. Heat oil in a medium saucepan over medium heat. Add onion, bell pepper, celery, salt, cumin, and pepper; cook and stir about 5 minutes, or until vegetables are softened. Add garlic; cook and stir 30 seconds. Add masa harina; cook, stirring continuously, about 3 minutes, or until light brown. Add broth and bay leaf; stir well. Bring to a boil. Reduce heat to low. Simmer, stirring occasionally, 10 minutes.
2. Add cilantro; stir well. Discard bay leaf. Set aside.
3. Fry tortilla strips. Heat oil in a medium skillet over medium heat. Fry tortilla strips, turning occasionally, 2 to 3 minutes, or until crisp and golden brown. Drain on paper towels.
4. Ladle soup into 4 serving bowls. Garnish each with avocado, cheese cubes, and tortilla strips. Serve immediately.

Yield: 4 Servings

Tip:

✓ See tip on page 13.

Salads and Salsas

Ensaladas y Salsas

Salads/Ensaladas

Salsas

Central American-Style Pickled Coleslaw
Curtido de Repollo

This is the Central American version of coleslaw. We serve it the same way traditional coleslaw is served in the United States. I use it as a topping for "Honduran-Style Enchiladas" (page 54), "Plantain Chips with Ground Beef" (page 59), and "Yucca with Pork Cracklings" (page 72) too.

1 (16-ounce) package coleslaw mix
1 teaspoon dried oregano leaves
$^1/_2$ teaspoon ground black pepper
$^1/_2$ cup distilled white vinegar
1 teaspoon salt
1 teaspoon sugar

1. Combine coleslaw mix, oregano, and pepper in a large glass or plastic bowl; toss well. Set aside.
2. Combine vinegar, salt, and sugar in a small glass or plastic bowl; stir until salt and sugar dissolve. Pour over coleslaw mixture. Toss to coat. Cover and refrigerate 30 minutes; toss before serving.

Yield: 4 Servings

Tropical Salad with Cilantro Vinaigrette
Ensalada Tropical con Vinagreta de Culantro

When I serve this salad, I like to begin with a "Piña Colada" (page 6) and end with "Pineapple Turnovers" (page 110) to keep the tropical theme from start to finish.

Cilantro Vinaigrette:
$1/_4$ cup extra virgin olive oil
2 tablespoons lime juice
$1/_4$ cup tightly packed cilantro leaves, finely chopped
$1/_2$ teaspoon salt
$1/_8$ teaspoon ground cayenne pepper

Salad:
8 cups tightly packed bite-size salad greens
$1/_4$ cup tightly packed cilantro leaves
1 (14-ounce) can hearts of palm, drained and cut into bite-size pieces
2 cups store-bought plantain chips
1 large ripe Hass avocado (see "tip"), pitted, peeled, and sliced
$1/_2$ cup diced dried pineapple

1. Prepare vinaigrette. Whisk all ingredients under "Cilantro Vinaigrette" in a small glass or plastic bowl until smooth. Set aside.
2. Divide salad greens, cilantro, hearts of palm, plantain chips, and avocado among 4 salad plates. Sprinkle each with 2 tablespoons pineapple. Serve with "Cilantro Vinaigrette" immediately.

Yield: 4 Servings

Tip:
   ✓   See tip on page 13.

Avocado and Mango Salsa
Salsa de Aguacate y Mango

This colorful salsa can add color and a tropical touch to any meal. I like to serve it with grilled seafood.

2 cups chopped tomato
1 cup chopped ripe Hass avocado (see "tip")
1 cup chopped ripe mango
1 jalapeño pepper, seeded and finely chopped
$^1/_2$ cup chopped red onion
$^1/_4$ cup cilantro leaves, chopped
$^1/_2$ teaspoon store-bought minced garlic
1 tablespoon lime juice
1 teaspoon olive oil
1 teaspoon distilled white vinegar
$^1/_2$ teaspoon salt
$^1/_4$ teaspoon ground black pepper

1. Combine all ingredients in a medium glass or plastic bowl; mix well. Cover and refrigerate 1 hour; stir before serving.

Yield: About 4$^1/_2$ Cups

Tip:

✓ See tip on page 13.

Central American-Style Salsa
Chimol

Chimol, also known as chirmol or chirimol, is the Central American version of the popular Mexican "Pico de Gallo" (page 36). It is traditionally served as an accompaniment for grilled meats, pork, and poultry.

3 cups chopped tomato
$^1/_2$ cup finely chopped green bell pepper
$^1/_2$ cup finely chopped red onion
$^1/_4$ cup cilantro leaves, chopped
$^1/_2$ teaspoon store-bought minced garlic
1 tablespoon lime juice
$^1/_2$ teaspoon distilled white vinegar
$^1/_2$ teaspoon salt
$^1/_4$ teaspoon ground black pepper

1. Combine all ingredients in a medium glass or plastic bowl; mix well. Cover and refrigerate 1 hour; stir before serving.

Yield: About 4 Cups

Chilean-Style Salsa
Pebre

*I think of pebre as the Chilean version of the Argentinean "Chimichurri" (page 118),
the Mexican "Pico de Gallo" (page 36), or the Central American "Chimol" (page 34).
The different versions of pebre are countless. This one comes from my mother, Jeanette.
Serve it with grilled meats, pork, or poultry.*

1 bunch cilantro, coarsely chopped
$1^1/_2$ cups chopped tomato
1 bunch green onions, thinly sliced
1 jalapeño pepper, seeded and finely chopped
1 teaspoon store-bought minced garlic
$^1/_4$ cup olive oil
2 tablespoons lime juice
$^1/_2$ teaspoon salt
Dash of ground black pepper
Pinch of ground cumin

1. Combine all ingredients in a medium glass or plastic bowl; mix well. Cover and
refrigerate 1 hour; stir before serving.

Yield: About $2^1/_2$ Cups

Pico de Gallo
Salsa Mexicana

A Mexican staple! To me, the green from the jalapeño and cilantro, the white from the white onion, and the red from the tomato represent the three colors of the Mexican flag (green, white, and red).

4 cups chopped tomato
1 cup chopped white onion
1 jalapeño pepper, seeded and chopped
$^1/_4$ cup cilantro leaves, chopped
$^1/_2$ teaspoon store-bought minced garlic
2 tablespoons lime juice
$^1/_2$ teaspoon salt

1. Combine all ingredients in a medium glass or plastic bowl; mix well. Cover and refrigerate 1 hour; stir before serving.

Yield: About 5 Cups

Main Dishes
Platos Principales

Main Dishes/Platos Principales

Argentinean-Style Grilled Beef Tenderloin
Churrasco

Churrasco is the word used by Argentineans to refer to grilled beef. The term has been widely adopted throughout the Caribbean and Latin America. Traditionally, it is served topped with "Chimichurri" (page 118). For a peppery change, I like to top it with "Jalapeño Sauce" (page 121) too. Serve it with a side of "Black Beans and Rice" (page 77) or "Red Beans and Rice" (page 89) and "Fried Sweet Plantains" (page 83) or "Plantain Patties" (page 88).

4 (about 8 ounces each) beef loin tenderloin steaks (also known as filet mignon steaks)
$^3/_4$ cup "Chimichurri" (see page 118), divided
Salt and ground black pepper

1. Holding a sharp knife parallel to the grain of one of the steaks, cut steak in a spiral motion into a long $^1/_2$-inch-thick strip. (see "illustration") Repeat with remaining steaks.
2. Combine steaks and $^1/_4$ cup of the "Chimichurri" sauce in a medium resealable plastic bag; seal bag. Turn to coat. Marinate in refrigerator 30 minutes to 1 hour.
3. Heat grill to high heat.
4. Remove steaks from refrigerator. Drain well. Discard marinade. Sprinkle both sides with salt and pepper.
5. Grill steaks 2 to 3 minutes per side for medium-rare or an additional 1 minute per side for medium. Serve with remaining $^1/_2$ cup "Chimichurri" sauce immediately.

Yield: 4 Churrascos

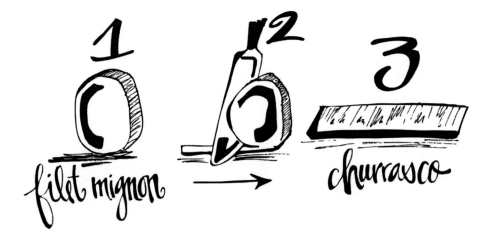

Baleadas

A Honduran staple! A baleada is a flour tortilla spread with "Refried Beans" (page 90) and "Honduran Cream" (page 120) and then folded in half to form a half-moon. Many refer to it as the Honduran burrito. It is served for breakfast, lunch, and dinner, or as a snack.

2 cups "Refried Beans" (see page 90), heated
$^1/_2$ cup "Honduran Cream" (see page 120)
8 (8-inch) soft taco-size flour tortillas, heated

1. Spread $^1/_4$ cup beans and 1 tablespoon cream on each tortilla. Fold in half to form a half-moon. Serve immediately.

Yield: 8 Baleadas

Beef Enchiladas
Enchiladas de Res

It's hard to imagine a Mexican menu without enchiladas. The different fillings are many. This is my personal favorite.

1 tablespoon canola oil
$^1/_2$ cup chopped yellow onion
$^1/_4$ cup chopped green bell pepper
$^1/_4$ cup chopped celery
$^1/_4$ teaspoon salt
$^1/_4$ teaspoon ground cayenne pepper
$^1/_4$ teaspoon ground cumin
1 pound ground beef
1 (7.76-ounce) can green Mexican salsa
8 (8-inch) soft taco-size flour tortillas
1 (10-ounce) can enchilada sauce
1 cup finely shredded Mexican cheese blend

1. Heat oil in a medium saucepan over medium heat. Add onion, bell pepper, celery, salt, pepper, and cumin; cook and stir about 5 minutes, or until vegetables are softened. Add meat; cook and stir 3 to 5 minutes, or until brown. Add green salsa; mix well. Cook, stirring occasionally, about 3 minutes, or until thoroughly heated. Set aside.
2. Heat oven to 350° F.
3. Grease a 13x9x2-inch baking pan with cooking spray. Set aside.
4. Top each tortilla with $^1/_3$ cup meat mixture. Roll up. Arrange, seam-side down, in greased baking pan.
5. Top enchiladas with enchilada sauce. Sprinkle with cheese.
6. Bake enchiladas about 20 minutes, or until thoroughly heated. Serve immediately.

Yield: 8 Enchiladas

Brazilian Black Bean and Meat Stew
Feijoada

Feijoada is to Brazilians what gumbo is to New Orleaneans. The different recipes for this meal are endless, since it can be made with numerous combinations of meats; yet, all are alike when it comes to the beans. I like to serve it with a side of "White Rice" (page 96).

1 (8-ounce) bag beef jerky, cut into bite-size pieces
1 tablespoon canola oil
1 cup chopped yellow onion
$^1/_2$ cup chopped green bell pepper
$^1/_2$ cup chopped celery
8 slices bacon, cut into $^1/_2$-inch pieces
1 pound fresh chorizo sausage, removed from casings and crumbled
$^1/_4$ teaspoon salt
$^1/_4$ teaspoon ground black pepper
1 tablespoon store-bought minced garlic
1 pound beef stew meat, tenderized
1 pound boneless country-style pork loin ribs
4 cups store-bought low-sodium beef broth, divided
1 bay leaf
3 (15-ounce) cans black beans, undrained, divided
1 tablespoon masa harina

1. Place beef jerky in a container. Add enough water to cover it; cover and refrigerate overnight.
2. Drain beef jerky. Set aside.
3. Heat oil in a large saucepan over medium heat. Add onion, bell pepper, celery, bacon, sausage, salt, and pepper; cook and stir 13 to 15 minutes, or until vegetables are softened. Add garlic; cook and stir 30 seconds. Add beef jerky, beef cubes, pork ribs, 2 cups of the broth, and bay leaf; stir well.
4. Place remaining 2 cups broth, beans from 1 of the cans, and masa harina in a blender. Cover and blend on high speed about 1 minute, or until smooth. Pour into saucepan; stir well. Bring to a boil. Reduce heat to low. Cook, stirring occasionally and skimming off excess fat that rises to the top, 1 hour and 45 minutes.
5. Add beans from remaining 2 cans; stir well. Cook, stirring occasionally, about 15 minutes, or until thoroughly heated. Discard bay leaf. Serve immediately.

Yield: 8 to 10 Servings

Chicken Chilaquiles with Green Salsa
Chilaquiles de Pollo con Salsa Verde

A Mexican classic! Store-bought tortilla chips and rotisserie chicken make this meal extremely easy and quick to assemble. The secret for perfect chilaquiles texture is to buy thick tortilla chips and to serve it as soon as it comes out of the oven. The longer it sits, the mushier the chips will get.

6 cups store-bought bite-size tortilla chips, divided
2 cups cooked shredded chicken (from a store-bought rotisserie chicken), divided
2 (7.76-ounce) cans green Mexican salsa, divided
1 cup crumbled cotija cheese (queso seco) or queso fresco

1. Heat oven to 350º F.
2. Grease an 8x8x2-inch baking pan with cooking spray. Make a layer with 3 cups of the chips; top with 1 cup of the chicken; top with green salsa from 1 of the cans. Repeat layers with remaining chips, chicken, and green salsa.
3. Bake chilaquiles about 15 minutes, or until thoroughly heated. Sprinkle with cheese. Serve immediately.

Yield: 4 Servings

Chicken Tacos
Tacos de Pollo

Tacos are to Mexicans what sandwiches are to Americans. As with sandwiches, tacos can be prepared with several fillings. Imagination is the limit. I chose to prepare mine with store-bought rotisserie chicken to keep it easy and simple.

2 tablespoons "Annatto Oil" (see page 117)
4 cups cooked shredded chicken (from a store-bought rotisserie chicken)
$^1/_4$ cup taco seasoning
$^1/_2$ cup store-bought low-sodium chicken broth
8 to 12 (6-inch) white corn tortillas, heated
"Guacamole" (see page 17), for serving
"Pico de Gallo" (see page 36), for serving

1. Heat oil in a medium saucepan over medium heat. Add chicken, taco seasoning, and broth; cook and stir about 3 minutes, or until thoroughly heated.
2. Serve chicken, tortillas, guacamole, and pico de gallo in individual platters immediately. Allow guests to fix their own tacos.

Yield: 8 to 12 Tacos

Chicken Tostadas
Tostadas de Pollo

Original to Mexico, tostadas are tortillas that are fried flat until crisp and then topped with different ingredients. Nowadays, store-bought tostada shells speed up the preparation process.

2 tablespoons olive oil
4 cups cooked shredded chicken (from a store-bought rotisserie chicken)
2 (7.76-ounce) cans green Mexican salsa
8 (5-inch) store-bought tostada shells, heated
2 cups "Refried Beans" (see page 90), heated
Finely shredded Mexican cheese blend

1. Heat oil in a medium skillet over medium heat. Add chicken and green salsa; cook and stir about 3 minutes, or until thoroughly heated. Set aside.

2. Arrange tostada shells on a large platter. Spread each with $1/4$ cup beans. Top each with $1/2$ cup chicken. Sprinkle each with cheese. Serve immediately.

Yield: 8 Tostadas

Chilean-Style Corn Pie
Pastel de Choclo

Pastel de choclo is a very typical dish in Chile. This and the following two recipes come from my mother, Jeanette. I like to serve it with a side of "Fried Sweet Plantains" (page 83).

Meat Layer:
3 cups "Chilean-Style Ground Beef" (see page 48), heated and drained

Raisins Layer:
1 (1.5-ounce) box raisins

Olive Layer:
1 (2.25-ounce) can sliced black olives, drained

Egg Layer:
4 hard-boiled eggs, peeled and sliced
Salt and ground black pepper

Corn Layer:
4 tablespoons unsalted butter
1 (1-pound) bag frozen yellow whole kernel corn, thawed
$^1/_2$ cup milk
1 tablespoon sugar
1 teaspoon cornstarch
$^1/_4$ teaspoon salt

$^1/_2$ teaspoon sugar, for sprinkling

1. Grease an 8x8x2-inch baking pan with cooking spray. Make a layer with the meat; sprinkle with raisins; sprinkle with olives; top with egg slices; sprinkle with salt and pepper. Set aside.
2. Heat oven to 350° F.
3. Prepare corn layer. Melt butter in a medium skillet over medium heat. Meanwhile, place corn, milk, sugar, cornstarch, and salt in a food processor. Cover and process about 1 minute, or until pureed. Pour into skillet. Cook, stirring continuously, about 5 minutes, or until slightly thicker. Spread evenly over egg layer. Sprinkle with sugar.
4. Bake corn pie about 15 minutes, or until thoroughly heated.
5. Broil until sugar is slightly brown. Let stand 5 minutes before serving.

Yield: 4 to 6 Servings

Chilean-Style Ground Beef
Pino Chileno

Pino is the traditional filling used in "Chilean Baked Turnovers" (page 14), "Chilean-Style Corn Pie" (page 47), and "Chilean-Style Potato Pie" (page 49). Try serving it over "White Rice" (page 96) or "Yellow Rice" (page 97) too.

2 tablespoons canola oil
1 cup chopped yellow onion
$^1/_2$ teaspoon salt
$^1/_2$ teaspoon dried oregano leaves
$^1/_4$ teaspoon ground cumin
$^1/_8$ teaspoon ground cayenne pepper
1 tablespoon store-bought minced garlic
1 pound ground beef
$^1/_4$ cup store-bought low-sodium chicken broth
1 teaspoon hot sauce

1. Heat oil in a medium saucepan over medium heat. Add onion, salt, oregano, cumin, and pepper; cook and stir about 5 minutes, or until onion is softened. Add garlic; cook and stir 30 seconds. Add meat; cook and stir 3 to 5 minutes, or until brown. Add broth and hot sauce; mix well. Bring to a boil. Reduce heat to low. Cook, stirring occasionally, 5 minutes. Serve immediately.

Yield: About 3 Cups

Chilean-Style Potato Pie
Pastel de Papas

I think of pastel de papas as having meat loaf with a side of mashed potatoes. Store-bought mashed potato mix makes this dish easy and fast to prepare.

Potato Layers:
1 (8-ounce) package mashed potatoes, plus ingredients to prepare mashed potatoes
$^1/_2$ cup grated Parmesan cheese

Meat Layer:
3 cups "Chilean-Style Ground Beef" (see page 48), heated and drained

Raisins Layer:
1 (1.5-ounce) box raisins

Olive Layer:
1 (2.25-ounce) can sliced black olives, drained

Egg Layer:
4 hard-boiled eggs, peeled and sliced
Salt and ground black pepper

Grated Parmesan cheese, for sprinkling

1. Prepare mashed potatoes as directed on package. Add cheese; mix well. Set aside.
2. Heat oven to 350° F.
3. Grease an 8x8x2-inch baking pan with cooking spray. Make a layer with $^1/_2$ of the mashed potatoes; top with meat; sprinkle with raisins; sprinkle with olives; top with egg slices; sprinkle with salt and pepper; top with remaining $^1/_2$ mashed potatoes. Sprinkle with cheese.
4. Bake potato pie about 15 minutes, or until thoroughly heated.
5. Broil 3 to 5 minutes, or until pie top is slightly brown. Let stand 5 minutes before serving.

Yield: 4 to 6 Servings

Cuban Sandwich
Emparedado Cubano

This is Cuba's most popular sandwich. Serve it with a side of "Fried Sweet Plantains" (page 83) or "Twice-Fried Green Plantains" (page 95).

4 tablespoons mustard
4 sub rolls, halved lengthwise
4 ($^{1}/_{4}$-inch thick) slices "Roasted Pork" (see page 65)
8 thin slices smoked ham
8 thin slices Swiss cheese
8 slices dill pickle
4 tablespoons unsalted butter, melted

1. Heat a nonstick griddle (comal) over medium heat.
2. Spread 1 tablespoon mustard on cut side of each roll. Top bottom part of rolls with 1 slice pork, 2 slices ham, 2 slices cheese, and 2 slices pickles. Top with top part of rolls. Brush both sides of each sandwich with butter.
3. Warm sandwiches on griddle, flattening with a large spatula, about 2 minutes per side, or until crusty and golden brown.
4. To serve, slice each sandwich in half on the diagonal.

Yield: 4 Sandwiches

Cuban-Style Ground Beef
Picadillo Cubano

I could not imagine a Cuban restaurant without picadillo on its menu. This is a signature dish of the Cuban cuisine. I like to serve it over a bed of "Yellow Rice" (page 97) and with a side of "Fried Sweet Plantains" (page 83) or to use it as a filling for "Cuban Picadillo Turnovers" (page 16).

2 tablespoons "Annatto Oil" (see page 117)
1 cup chopped yellow onion
$^1/_2$ cup chopped green bell pepper
$^1/_2$ cup chopped celery
$^1/_2$ teaspoon dried oregano leaves
$^1/_2$ teaspoon salt
$^1/_4$ teaspoon ground cumin
$^1/_4$ teaspoon ground cayenne pepper
1 tablespoon store-bought minced garlic
1 pound ground beef
1 (8-ounce) can tomato sauce
$^1/_2$ cup store-bought low-sodium chicken broth
1 tablespoon red-wine vinegar
$^1/_2$ cup sliced pimiento-stuffed olives
1 (1.5-ounce) box raisins
$^1/_8$ teaspoon sugar

1. Heat oil in a medium saucepan over medium heat. Add onion, bell pepper, celery, oregano, salt, cumin, and pepper; cook and stir about 5 minutes, or until vegetables are softened. Add garlic; cook and stir 30 seconds. Add meat; cook and stir 3 to 5 minutes, or until brown. Add tomato sauce, broth, vinegar, olives, raisins, and sugar; mix well. Bring to a boil. Reduce heat to low. Cook, stirring occasionally, 15 minutes. Serve immediately.

Yield: About 4 Cups

Cuban-Style Shredded Beef
Ropa Vieja

"Ropa vieja" literally translates to "old clothes" in English. It was named this way due to the resemblance shredded beef has with ragged clothes. Traditionally, it is served over a bed of "White Rice" (page 96) and a side of "Fried Sweet Plantains" (page 83).

To cook the steak:
2 pounds skirt steak, excess fat trimmed off
2 stalks celery, cut into 1-inch pieces
2 bay leaves
1 medium tomato, quartered
1 medium yellow onion, quartered
1 green bell pepper, seeded and cut into 1-inch pieces
8 cups water

To prepare the dish:
2 tablespoons "Annatto Oil" (see page 117)
2 medium yellow onions, julienned
1 green bell pepper, seeded and julienned
1 teaspoon salt
$^1/_2$ teaspoon ground cumin
$^1/_8$ teaspoon ground cayenne pepper
1 (8-ounce) can tomato sauce
$^1/_2$ cup sliced pimiento-stuffed olives
Pinch of sugar

1. Combine all ingredients under "To cook the steak" in a large saucepan. Bring to a boil over medium heat. Reduce heat to low. Cover and cook, stirring occasionally and skimming off scum that rises to the top, 2 hours.
2. Strain meat, reserving 2 cups broth.
3. Shred meat by pulling it apart with two forks. Set aside.
4. Heat oil in a large skillet over medium heat. Add onion, bell pepper, salt, cumin, and pepper; cook and stir about 5 minutes, or until vegetables are softened. Add cooked shredded meat, 2 cups reserved broth, tomato sauce, olives, and sugar; mix well. Bring to a boil. Reduce heat to low. Simmer, stirring occasionally, 15 minutes. Serve immediately.

Yield: 6 Servings

Honduran Breakfast Burrito
Burrita

"Burrita", which literally translates to "baby female donkey", is a very typical Honduran meal served mainly for breakfast; however, some serve it for lunch and dinner as well. Unlike the Mexican burrito, which is folded on one end and then rolled, the Honduran burrita is folded in half to form a half-moon. This is the way my friend Waldina prepares hers.

1 cup "Refried Beans" (see page 90), heated
$^1/_4$ cup "Honduran Cream" (see page 120)
4 (8-inch) soft taco-size flour tortillas, heated
4 large eggs, scrambled
$^1/_4$ cup finely shredded Mexican cheese blend

1. Spread $^1/_4$ cup beans and 1 tablespoon cream on each tortilla. Top each with 1 egg. Sprinkle each with 1 tablespoon cheese. Fold in half to form a half-moon. Serve immediately.

Yield: 4 Burritas

Honduran-Style Enchiladas
Enchiladas Hondureñas

Enchiladas Hondureñas are to Hondurans what tostadas are to Mexicans. As with "Chicken Tostadas" (page 46), using store-bought tostada shells cuts down the assembling time. This is how my Honduran aunt Angelica Diaz de Yacaman taught me to make them.

8 (5-inch) store-bought tostada shells, heated
4 cups "Honduran-Style Ground Beef" (see page 55), heated and drained
4 cups "Central American-Style Pickled Coleslaw" (see page 31)
$^1/_2$ cup "Tomato Sauce" (see page 122), heated
2 hard-boiled eggs, peeled and sliced
Grated Parmesan cheese

1. Arrange tostada shells on a large platter. Top each with $^1/_2$ cup meat, $^1/_2$ cup coleslaw, and 1 tablespoon tomato sauce. Divide egg slices among enchiladas. Sprinkle each with cheese. Serve immediately.

Yield: 8 Enchiladas

Honduran-Style Ground Beef
Picadillo Hondureño

I use this recipe for "Honduran-Style Enchiladas" (page 54) and "Plantain Chips with Ground Beef" (page 59). Also, I like to serve it over a bed of "White Rice" (page 96).

2 tablespoons "Annatto Oil" (see page 117) or canola oil
1 cup chopped yellow onion
$^1/_2$ cup chopped green bell pepper
$^1/_2$ teaspoon salt
$^1/_4$ teaspoon ground cumin
$^1/_4$ teaspoon ground cayenne pepper
1 tablespoon store-bought minced garlic
1 pound ground beef
$^1/_4$ cup store-bought low-sodium chicken broth
1 (14.5-ounce) can diced new potatoes, drained

1. Heat oil in a medium saucepan over medium heat. Add onion, bell pepper, salt, cumin, and pepper; cook and stir about 5 minutes, or until vegetables are softened. Add garlic; cook and stir 30 seconds. Add meat; cook and stir 3 to 5 minutes, or until brown. Add broth and potatoes; mix well. Reduce heat to low. Cook, stirring occasionally, 15 minutes. Serve immediately.

Yield: About 4 Cups

Mexican Pork and Hominy Stew
Pozole

A Mexican classic! It makes a great dish for any celebration. Serve it with a side of "Cilantro Rice" (page 78) and "Pickled Onions" (page 87).

1 teaspoon "Annatto Oil" (see page 117) or canola oil
1 cup chopped yellow onion
1 jalapeño or serrano pepper, seeded and chopped
4 slices bacon, cut into $^1/_2$-inch pieces
$^1/_4$ teaspoon salt
$^1/_8$ teaspoon ground cayenne pepper
1 tablespoon store-bought minced garlic
1 tablespoon masa harina
1 pound boneless pork stew meat
2 (15.5-ounce) cans white hominy, drained
4 cups store-bought low-sodium chicken broth
1 bay leaf

1. Heat oil in a medium saucepan over medium heat. Add onion, pepper, bacon, salt, and pepper; cook and stir 8 to 10 minutes, or until vegetables are softened and bacon starts to crisp. Add garlic; cook and stir 30 seconds. Add masa harina; cook, stirring continuously, 30 seconds. Add pork cubes, hominy, broth, and bay leaf; stir well. Bring to a boil. Reduce heat to low. Cook, stirring occasionally and skimming off excess fat that rises to the top, 1 hour.
2. Remove saucepan from heat. Discard bay leaf. Serve immediately.

Yield: 4 Servings

Mexican-Style Lasagna
Pastel Azteca

Pastel azteca is to Mexicans what lasagna is to Italians or what moussaka is to Greeks. It is layered like a traditional lasagna and spiced with Mexican flavors, which makes this dish an interesting and exceptional meal for any get-together.

3 tablespoons canola oil
1 cup chopped yellow onion
$^1/_2$ cup chopped green bell pepper
$^1/_2$ cup chopped celery
1 tablespoon store-bought minced garlic
1 pound ground beef
1 (1.25-ounce) package taco seasoning mix
$^1/_3$ cup store-bought low-sodium chicken broth
Vegetable oil, for frying tortillas
8 (6-inch) white corn tortillas
8 slices American cheese, divided
2 cups shredded mozzarella cheese, divided

1. Heat canola oil in a medium saucepan over medium heat. Add onion, bell pepper, and celery; cook and stir about 5 minutes, or until vegetables are softened. Add garlic; cook and stir 30 seconds. Add meat; cook and stir 3 to 5 minutes, or until brown. Add taco seasoning and broth; mix well. Cook, stirring occasionally, about 3 minutes, or until thoroughly heated. Set aside.
2. Fry tortillas. Heat vegetable oil in a medium skillet over medium heat. Slightly fry each tortilla 5 seconds per side. Set aside.
3. Heat oven to 350° F.
4. Grease an 8x8x2-inch baking pan with cooking spray. Make a layer with 4 of the tortillas; top with 4 of the American cheese slices; top with $^1/_2$ of the meat mixture; top with 1 cup of the mozzarella cheese. Repeat layers with remaining tortillas, American cheese slices, meat mixture, and mozzarella cheese. Cover with aluminum foil.
5. Bake lasagna about 10 minutes, or until thoroughly heated.
6. Remove baking pan from oven. Carefully remove foil. Return to oven. Broil until cheese is melted and slightly brown. Let stand 5 minutes before serving.

Yield: 4 to 6 Servings

Paella

Paella is to Spaniards what jambalaya is to Louisianans. This Spanish dish has been adopted throughout the Caribbean and Latin America. The recipes for this meal are endless. I like to add yellow coloring powder (amarillo), found in the spice section of Latin markets or large supermarkets, to my version to give it its intense bright color; yet, if you are unable to find the powder, don't worry, since this will not change its taste a bit.

3 tablespoons olive oil
1 pound fresh chorizo sausage, removed from casings and crumbled
1 cup chopped yellow onion
$^{1}/_{2}$ cup chopped green bell pepper
$^{1}/_{2}$ cup chopped celery
1 teaspoon salt
$^{1}/_{2}$ teaspoon yellow coloring powder (amarillo) (optional)
$^{1}/_{4}$ teaspoon ground cayenne pepper
3 tablespoons store-bought minced garlic
2 boneless, skinless chicken breasts, cut into 1-inch cubes
3 cups long-grain white rice
1 (10-ounce) can diced tomatoes with green chiles, undrained
6 cups store-bought low-sodium chicken broth
1 teaspoon saffron threads
1 (1-pound) bag frozen raw, peeled, and deveined medium shrimp, thawed
1 (8.5-ounce) can sweet peas, drained

1. Heat oil in a large saucepan over medium heat. Add sausage, onion, bell pepper, celery, salt, coloring (if using), and pepper; cook and stir about 12 minutes, or until sausage is brown and vegetables are softened. Add garlic; cook and stir 30 seconds. Add chicken; cook and stir about 3 minutes, or until no longer pink. Add rice; stir until rice grains look coated with oil. Add tomatoes, broth, and saffron; mix well. Bring to a boil. Reduce heat to low. Cover and cook 18 minutes.
2. Add shrimp and peas; gently mix well. Cover and cook about 8 minutes, or until shrimp turn pink and most of the liquid is absorbed.
3. Remove saucepan from heat. Let stand, covered, 5 minutes. Fluff rice with a fork. Serve immediately.

Yield: 8 to 12 Servings

Plantain Chips with Ground Beef
Tajaditas de Plátano con Carne

An all-time Honduran favorite! Many serve a smaller portion as a snack; however, I like it so much that I would rather serve a larger portion to make it a meal.

4 cups store-bought plantain chips
4 cups "Central American-Style Pickled Coleslaw" (see page 31)
4 cups "Honduran-Style Ground Beef" (see page 55), heated and drained
$^1/_2$ cup "Tomato Sauce" (see page 122), heated
Grated Parmesan cheese

1. Place 1 cup plantain chips on 4 individual plates. Top each with 1 cup coleslaw, 1 cup meat, and 2 tablespoons tomato sauce. Sprinkle each with cheese. Serve immediately.

Yield: 4 Servings

Puerto Rican Chicken Stew
Asopao de Pollo

A Puerto Rican staple! I like to think of this dish as a cross between chicken soup and "Rice with Chicken" (page 61). This recipe comes from my Puerto Rican sister-in-law Michelle Marin de Yibrin. Serve it with a side of "Twice-Fried Green Plantains" (page 95).

1 tablespoon "Annatto Oil" (see page 117)
$^1/_2$ cup chopped yellow onion
$^1/_4$ cup chopped green bell pepper
$^1/_4$ cup chopped celery
$^1/_2$ teaspoon salt
$^1/_4$ teaspoon ground cayenne pepper
2 boneless, skinless chicken breasts, cut into 1-inch cubes
1 cup medium-grain white rice
1 (10-ounce) can diced tomatoes with green chiles, undrained
1 (8-ounce) can tomato sauce
6 cups store-bought low-sodium chicken broth
1 bay leaf
Pinch of sugar
1 (8.5-ounce) can sweet peas, drained

1. Heat oil in a medium saucepan over medium heat. Add onion, bell pepper, celery, salt, and pepper; cook and stir about 5 minutes, or until vegetables are softened. Add chicken; cook and stir about 3 minutes, or until no longer pink. Add rice; stir until rice grains look coated with oil. Add tomatoes, tomato sauce, broth, bay leaf, and sugar; stir well. Bring to a boil. Reduce heat to low. Cover and cook 15 minutes.
2. Add peas; gently stir well. Cover and cook 5 minutes. Discard bay leaf. Serve immediately.

Yield: 4 to 6 Servings

Rice with Chicken
Arroz con Pollo

Annatto oil and yellow coloring gives arroz con pollo its distinctive flavor and bright color. While each Caribbean and Latin American country has its own version, most are similar and equally delicious. This is my version.

2 tablespoons "Annatto Oil" (see page 117)
$^1/_2$ cup chopped yellow onion
$^1/_4$ cup chopped green bell pepper
$^1/_4$ cup chopped celery
$^1/_2$ teaspoon salt
$^1/_4$ teaspoon ground cumin
$^1/_8$ teaspoon ground cayenne pepper
1 tablespoon store-bought minced garlic
2 boneless, skinless chicken breasts, cut into 1-inch cubes
1 cup long-grain white rice
1 (10-ounce) can diced tomatoes with green chiles, undrained
$^1/_2$ cup sliced pimiento-stuffed olives
1 bay leaf
1 teaspoon dried oregano leaves
$^1/_4$ teaspoon yellow coloring powder (amarillo) (optional)
2 cups store-bought low-sodium chicken broth
1 (8.5-ounce) can sweet peas, drained

1. Heat oil in a medium saucepan over medium heat. Add onion, bell pepper, celery, salt, cumin, and pepper; cook and stir about 5 minutes, or until vegetables are softened. Add garlic; cook and stir 30 seconds. Add chicken; cook and stir about 3 minutes, or until no longer pink. Add rice; stir until rice grains look coated with oil. Add tomatoes, olives, bay leaf, oregano, coloring (if using), and broth; mix well. Bring to a boil. Reduce heat to low. Cover and cook 18 minutes.
2. Add peas; gently mix well. Cover and cook about 5 minutes, or until most of the liquid is absorbed.
3. Remove saucepan from heat. Let stand, covered, 5 minutes. Fluff rice with a fork. Discard bay leaf. Serve immediately.

Yield: 4 to 6 Servings

Rice with Chorizo
Arroz con Chorizo

Chorizo is a highly seasoned pork sausage used throughout Latin America. It can be found fresh or smoked in Latin markets or large supermarkets. This recipe calls for fresh chorizo sausage, which gives this dish its distinctive taste.

2 tablespoons "Annatto Oil" (see page 117) or canola oil
1 pound fresh chorizo sausage, removed from casings and crumbled
$^1/_2$ cup chopped yellow onion
$^1/_4$ cup chopped green bell pepper
$^1/_4$ cup chopped celery
$^1/_4$ teaspoon salt
$^1/_4$ teaspoon ground cayenne pepper
$^1/_4$ teaspoon ground cumin
1 tablespoon store-bought minced garlic
1 cup long-grain white rice
1 (10-ounce) can diced tomatoes with green chiles, undrained
2 cups store-bought low-sodium chicken broth
1 bay leaf
1 (8.5-ounce) can sweet peas, drained

1. Heat oil in a medium saucepan over medium heat. Add sausage, onion, bell pepper, celery, salt, pepper, and cumin; cook and stir about 12 minutes, or until sausage is brown and vegetables are softened. Add garlic; cook and stir 30 seconds. Add rice; stir until rice grains look coated with oil. Add tomatoes, broth, and bay leaf; mix well. Bring to a boil. Reduce heat to low. Cover and cook 18 minutes.
2. Add peas; gently mix well. Cover and cook about 5 minutes, or until most of the liquid is absorbed.
3. Remove saucepan from heat. Let stand, covered, 5 minutes. Fluff rice with a fork. Discard bay leaf. Serve immediately.

Yield: 4 to 6 Servings

Rice with Shrimp
Arroz con Camarones

The ingredients used to make this dish vary from country to country throughout the Caribbean and Latin America; however, most are alike. Store-bought peeled and deveined shrimp will save you a lot of time. Serve it with a side of "Fried Sweet Plantains" (page 83).

2 tablespoons "Annatto Oil" (see page 117) or canola oil
$^1/_2$ cup chopped yellow onion
$^1/_4$ cup chopped green bell pepper
$^1/_4$ cup chopped celery
$^1/_2$ teaspoon salt
$^1/_4$ teaspoon ground cumin
$^1/_8$ teaspoon ground cayenne pepper
1 tablespoon store-bought minced garlic
1 cup long-grain white rice
1 (10-ounce) can diced tomatoes with green chiles, undrained
2 cups store-bought low-sodium chicken broth
1 bay leaf
$^1/_2$ teaspoon dried oregano leaves
$^1/_4$ teaspoon yellow coloring powder (amarillo) (optional)
1 (1-pound) bag frozen raw, peeled, and deveined medium shrimp, thawed
1 (8.5-ounce) can sweet peas, drained
Lime wedges, for serving

1. Heat oil in a medium saucepan over medium heat. Add onion, bell pepper, celery, salt, cumin, and pepper; cook and stir about 5 minutes, or until vegetables are softened. Add garlic; cook and stir 30 seconds. Add rice; stir until rice grains look coated with oil. Add tomatoes, broth, bay leaf, oregano, and coloring (if using); mix well. Bring to a boil. Reduce heat to low. Cover and cook 18 minutes.
2. Add shrimp and peas; gently mix well. Cover and cook about 8 minutes, or until shrimp turn pink and most of the liquid is absorbed.
3. Remove saucepan from heat. Let stand, covered, 5 minutes. Fluff rice with a fork. Discard bay leaf. Serve with lime wedges immediately.

Yield: 4 to 6 Servings

Rice with Squid
Arroz con Calamares

The ink sauce in canned squid gives this rice its distinctive color and flavor. You can find squid in ink sauce (calamares en su tinta) cans in Latin markets or large supermarkets.

1 tablespoon olive oil
$^1/_2$ cup chopped yellow onion
$^1/_4$ cup chopped green bell pepper
$^1/_4$ cup chopped celery
$^1/_4$ teaspoon salt
$^1/_8$ teaspoon ground cayenne pepper
1 tablespoon store-bought minced garlic
1 cup long-grain white rice
2 (4-ounce) cans squid in ink sauce, undrained
2 cups store-bought low-sodium chicken broth
1 bay leaf
Lime wedges, for serving

1. Heat oil in a medium saucepan over medium heat. Add onion, bell pepper, celery, salt, and pepper; cook and stir about 5 minutes, or until vegetables are softened. Add garlic; cook and stir 30 seconds. Add rice; stir until rice grains look coated with oil. Add squid, broth, and bay leaf; mix well. Bring to a boil. Reduce heat to low. Cover and cook about 15 minutes, or until most of the liquid is absorbed.
2. Remove saucepan from heat. Let stand, covered, 5 minutes. Discard bay leaf. Fluff rice with a fork. Serve with lime wedges immediately.

Yield: 4 Servings

Roasted Pork
Lechón Asado/Pernil al Horno

Roasted pork is a very popular dish in Cuba and Puerto Rico. It is traditionally cooked for the holidays and served with a side of "Black Beans and Rice" (page 77) in Cuba, "Rice with Pigeon Peas" (page 92) in Puerto Rico, and "Fried Sweet Plantains" (page 83) or "Twice-Fried Green Plantains" (page 95). I like to serve it with a side of "Cuban Garlic Sauce" (page 119) or "Jalapeño Sauce" (page 121), too.

$1/_4$ cup olive oil
1 tablespoon lime juice
4 cloves garlic
1 teaspoon dried oregano leaves
1 teaspoon salt
$1/_2$ teaspoon ground black pepper
$1/_2$ teaspoon ground cumin
1 (about 3 $1/_2$ pounds) boneless pork loin roast

1. Place oil, lime juice, garlic, oregano, salt, pepper, and cumin in a food processor. Cover and process about 30 seconds, or until smooth.
2. Combine garlic marinade and pork in a large resealable plastic bag; seal bag. Turn to coat. Refrigerate overnight.
3. Heat oven to 350º F.
4. Roast pork, uncovered, in a roasting pan for 1 hour.
5. Remove roasting pan from oven. Carefully loosely cover pan with aluminum foil. Return to oven. Roast an additional 30 minutes, or until no longer pink in center and internal temperature reaches 170º F. Let stand, covered, 10 minutes before slicing and serving.

Yield: 6 to 8 Servings

Spanish Chick Pea and Chorizo Stew
Cazuela de Garbanzos y Chorizo

Original to Spain, this stew has been widely adopted in several Latin American countries. Serve it with a side of "White Rice" (page 96) or "Yellow Rice" (page 97).

1 teaspoon olive oil
1 pound fresh chorizo sausage, removed from casings and crumbled
1 cup chopped yellow onion
$^1/_4$ teaspoon salt
$^1/_8$ teaspoon ground cayenne pepper
1 tablespoon store-bought minced garlic
2 (16-ounce) cans chick peas, drained
1 (8-ounce) can tomato sauce
3 cups store-bought low-sodium chicken broth
1 bay leaf
Pinch of sugar

1. Heat oil in a medium saucepan over medium heat. Add sausage, onion, salt, and pepper; cook and stir about 10 minutes, or until sausage is brown and onion is softened. Add garlic; cook and stir 30 seconds. Add chick peas, tomato sauce, broth, bay leaf, and sugar; stir well. Bring to a boil. Reduce heat to low. Simmer, stirring occasionally and skimming off excess fat that rises to the top, 10 minutes.
2. Remove saucepan from heat. Discard bay leaf. Serve immediately.

Yield: 4 to 6 Servings

Spanish-Style Garlic Shrimp
Camarones al Ajillo

Ole! Original to Spain, this dish has become a favorite in the Caribbean and Latin America. Serve it with a side of "Coconut Rice" (page 79) or "White Rice" (page 96).

$^1/_2$ **cup olive oil**
$^1/_4$ **cup store-bought minced garlic**
$^1/_2$ **teaspoon paprika**
$^1/_4$ **teaspoon ground cayenne pepper**
1 (1-pound) bag frozen raw, peeled, and deveined extra large shrimp, tails on, thawed
$^1/_2$ **teaspoon salt**
$^1/_4$ **cup finely chopped parsley**
Lime wedges, for serving

1. Heat oil in a large skillet over medium heat. Add garlic, paprika, and pepper; cook and stir 2 minutes. Add shrimp and salt; cook and stir about 4 minutes, or until shrimp turn pink. Remove from heat. Add parsley; mix well. Serve with lime wedges immediately.

Yield: 4 Servings

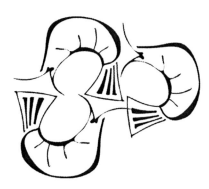

Spanish-Style Omelet
Tortilla Española

Tortilla Española is to Spaniards what omelet is to French or what frittata is to Italians. While many think of it as a breakfast meal, in Latin America it is served for breakfast, lunch, or dinner.

8 large eggs
$^1/_2$ teaspoon salt
2 tablespoons olive oil
1 cup chopped yellow onion
$^1/_2$ cup chopped green bell pepper
1 (14.5-ounce) can diced new potatoes, drained
$^1/_2$ teaspoon paprika
$^1/_2$ teaspoon ground cayenne pepper

1. Heat oven to 375º F.
2. Whisk eggs and salt in a medium bowl until well blended. Set aside.
3. Heat oil in a 10-inch nonstick, ovenproof skillet over medium heat. Add onion, bell pepper, potatoes, paprika, and pepper; cook and stir about 7 minutes, or until vegetables are softened.
4. Stir egg mixture. Pour over potato mixture. Cook, without stirring, 3 minutes.
5. Transfer skillet into oven. Bake about 12 minutes, or until eggs are set.
6. Remove skillet from oven. Let stand 3 minutes. Invert omelet onto a serving platter. Cut into 4 wedges. Serve immediately.

Yield: 4 Servings

Venezuelan-Style Corn Pancakes
Cachapas

A Venezuelan favorite! Many think of pancakes as a breakfast meal; however, this version can be served for any meal. Asadero cheese, found in Latin markets or large supermarkets, is a great melting cheese to complement cachapas. This recipe was inspired by my Venezuelan friend Miguel's recipe. I like to serve them with a side of "Black Beans" (page 76) and "Fried Sweet Plantains" (page 83).

1 (15.25-ounce) can yellow whole kernel corn, undrained
1 (5.5-ounce) package pancake mix
$^1/_2$ cup water
Canola oil, for cooking cachapas
5 slices asadero cheese

1. Drain corn, reserving $^1/_2$ cup liquid.
2. Place reserved $^1/_2$ cup corn liquid, corn, pancake mix, and water in a blender. Cover and blend on low speed 1 minute. Stop blender; scrape sides. Cover and blend on high speed an additional 30 seconds, or until smooth.
3. Heat a nonstick griddle (comal) over medium heat.
4. Brush griddle with oil. Pour a heaping $^1/_2$ cup corn mixture onto griddle. Cook cachapa about 2 minutes per side, or until dark golden brown. Immediately top with 1 slice cheese. Fold in half to form a half-moon. Serve immediately. Repeat with remaining corn mixture.

Yield: 5 Cachapas

Venezuelan-Style Shredded Beef
Pabellón Criollo

"Pabellón Criollo" literally translates to "flag creole" in English. The name is due to the resemblance this dish has with the Venezuelan flag—both are composed of three different colors. The components of this dish are shredded beef, black beans, and white rice; thus, making the meal tricolor. In contrast, the Venezuelan flag has three colors (yellow, blue, and red) too. Serve it with a side of "Fried Sweet Plantains" (page 83).

To cook the steak:
2 pounds skirt steak, excess fat trimmed off
2 stalks celery, cut into 1-inch pieces
2 bay leaves
1 medium tomato, quartered
1 medium yellow onion, quartered
1 green bell pepper, seeded and cut into 1-inch pieces
8 cups water

To prepare the shredded beef:
2 tablespoons "Annatto Oil" (see page 117)
$^1/_2$ cup chopped yellow onion
$^1/_4$ cup chopped green bell pepper
$^1/_4$ cup chopped celery
$^1/_2$ teaspoon salt
$^1/_4$ teaspoon ground cayenne pepper
1 tablespoon store-bought minced garlic
1 (8-ounce) can tomato sauce
Pinch of sugar

"Black Beans" (see page 76), for serving, heated
"White Rice" (see page 96), for serving, heated
"Fried Sweet Plantains" (see page 83), for serving, heated

1. Combine all ingredients under "To cook the steak" in a large saucepan. Bring to a boil over medium heat. Reduce heat to low. Cover and cook, stirring occasionally and skimming off scum that rises to the top, 2 hours.
2. Strain meat, reserving 1 cup broth.
3. Shred meat by pulling it apart with two forks. Set aside.

4. Heat oil in a large skillet over medium heat. Add onion, bell pepper, celery, salt, and pepper; cook and stir about 5 minutes, or until vegetables are softened. Add garlic; cook and stir 30 seconds. Add cooked shredded meat, 1 cup reserved broth, tomato sauce, and sugar; mix well. Bring to a boil. Reduce heat to low. Simmer, stirring occasionally, 15 minutes.
5. Serve shredded beef, black beans, white rice, and fried sweet plantains on individual platters immediately. Allow guests to fix their own pabellón.

Yield: 6 Servings

Yucca with Pork Cracklings
Yuca con Chicharron

Yucca's starchy texture makes me think of it as the Latin American substitute for potatoes. This dish has been an all-time favorite throughout Central America.

2 pounds yucca, peeled and cut crosswise into 3- to 4-inch pieces
1 tablespoon salt
4 cups "Central American-Style Pickled Coleslaw" (see page 31)
$^1/_4$ pound store-bought pork cracklings or 1 (4-ounce) bag pork cracklings (see "tip")
$^1/_2$ cup "Tomato Sauce" (see page 122), heated
Grated Parmesan cheese

1. Place yucca in a large saucepan. Add salt and enough water to cover it by 1 inch; bring to a boil over high heat. Reduce heat to medium. Cook 15 to 18 minutes, or until fork-tender. Drain well. Cool to the touch.
2. Cut yucca pieces in half, lengthwise; remove and discard stringy fibers from the center.
3. Arrange yucca on a large platter. Top with coleslaw, pork cracklings, and tomato sauce. Sprinkle with cheese. Serve immediately.

Yield: 4 Servings

Tip:

✓ See tip on page 25.

Side Dishes

Acompañamientos

Side Dishes/Acompañamientos

Black Beans
Frijoles Negros

As a Latino, I could not imagine going a week without eating beans. The different types consumed in Latin America vary from country to country. This particular recipe calls for black beans but will taste equally delicious with any type of beans.

1 tablespoon olive oil
$^1/_2$ cup chopped yellow onion
$^1/_4$ cup chopped green bell pepper
$^1/_4$ cup chopped celery
$^1/_4$ teaspoon salt
$^1/_8$ teaspoon ground cayenne pepper
1 tablespoon store-bought minced garlic
1 (15-ounce) can black beans, undrained
$^1/_2$ cup store-bought low-sodium chicken broth
$^1/_4$ cup cilantro leaves, coarsely chopped

1. Heat oil in a medium skillet over medium heat. Add onion, bell pepper, celery, salt, and pepper; cook and stir about 5 minutes, or until vegetables are softened. Add garlic; cook and stir 30 seconds. Add beans and broth; mix well. Bring to a boil. Reduce heat to low. Simmer, stirring occasionally, 10 minutes.
2. Remove saucepan from heat. Add cilantro; mix well. Serve immediately.

Yield: 4 Servings

Black Beans and Rice
Moros y Cristianos

A Cuban classic! "Moros y Cristianos" literally translates to "Moors and Christians" in English. It was named this way due to the resemblance the combination of the black beans and the white rice had with the racial make up of the immigrants who came from the Old World and settled in Cuba.

1 tablespoon olive oil
$^1/_2$ cup chopped yellow onion
$^1/_4$ cup chopped green bell pepper
$^1/_4$ cup chopped celery
$^1/_2$ teaspoon salt
Pinch of ground cayenne pepper
1 tablespoon store-bought minced garlic
1 cup long-grain white rice
1 (15-ounce) can black beans, undrained
2 cups store-bought low-sodium chicken broth
1 bay leaf

1. Heat oil in a medium saucepan over medium heat. Add onion, bell pepper, celery, salt, and pepper; cook and stir about 5 minutes, or until vegetables are softened. Add garlic; cook and stir 30 seconds. Add rice; stir until rice grains look coated with oil. Add beans, broth, and bay leaf; mix well. Bring to a boil. Reduce heat to low. Cover and cook 17 to 20 minutes, or until most of the liquid is absorbed.
2. Remove saucepan from heat. Let stand, covered, 5 minutes. Fluff rice with a fork. Discard bay leaf. Serve immediately.

Yield: 4 to 6 Servings

Cilantro Rice
Arroz con Culantro

Cilantro is one of the most widely used herbs in the Caribbean and Latin America. It adds a refreshing taste and colorful touch to this rice. Serve it as a side to brighten up your meals.

1 tablespoon canola oil
1 cup long-grain white rice
$^1/_4$ teaspoon salt
2 cups store-bought low-sodium chicken broth, divided
$^1/_2$ cup cilantro leaves

1. Heat oil in a medium saucepan over medium heat. Add rice and salt; stir until rice grains look coated with oil. Add 1 cup of the broth; mix well.
2. Place remaining 1 cup broth and cilantro in a blender. Cover and blend on low speed about 30 seconds, or until smooth. Pour into saucepan; mix well. Bring to a boil. Reduce heat to low. Cover and cook about 15 minutes, or until most of the liquid is absorbed.
3. Remove saucepan from heat. Let stand, covered, 5 minutes. Fluff rice with a fork. Serve immediately.

Yield: 4 Servings

Coconut Rice
Arroz con Coco

The sweetness from the coconut water used for this recipe adds an exceptional taste to this rice. It's a perfect complement to any seafood dish.

1 tablespoon canola oil
1 cup long-grain white rice
$^1/_2$ teaspoon salt
$^1/_4$ teaspoon ground white pepper
2 cups store-bought coconut water

1. Heat oil in a medium saucepan over medium heat. Add rice, salt, and pepper; stir until rice grains look coated with oil. Add coconut water; mix well. Bring to a boil. Reduce heat to low. Cover and cook about 15 minutes, or until most of the liquid is absorbed.
2. Remove saucepan from heat. Let stand, covered, 5 minutes. Fluff rice with a fork. Serve immediately.

Yield: 4 Servings

Corn Patties
Tortitas de Maíz

These patties are my sweet version of the wonderful Colombian and Venezuelan "Arepas" (page 82).

1 (8.75-ounce) can yellow whole kernel corn, drained
1 cup plain bread crumbs
2 tablespoons sugar
Pinch of ground cinnamon
2 tablespoons unsalted butter, melted
1 large egg
Vegetable oil, for frying patties

1. Place corn in a food processor. Cover and process about 30 seconds, or until pureed. Set aside.
2. Combine bread crumbs, sugar, and cinnamon in a medium bowl; mix well. Add corn puree, butter, and egg; mix well. Let stand 5 minutes.
3. Form corn mixture into 8 patties, 3-inch in diameter by $^1/_4$-inch thick. Place on a wax paper-lined tray. Cover with plastic wrap and refrigerate 1 hour.
4. Pour oil into a medium nonstick skillet to a depth of $^1/_4$-inch; heat over medium heat.
5. Fry patties about 2 minutes per side, or until golden brown. Drain on paper towels. Serve immediately.

Yield: 4 Servings

Corn Soufflé
Soufflé de Choclo

This yummy soufflé has been a classic in my parents' house for years. Its sweetness complements any savory dish. This recipe comes from my mother, Jeanette.

3 large eggs
1 (15.25-ounce) can yellow whole kernel corn, drained
1 (14-ounce) can sweetened condensed milk
$^1/_2$ cup (1 stick) unsalted butter, melted
$^1/_4$ cup all-purpose flour
Pinch of salt

1. Heat oven to 350º F.
2. Grease an 8x8x2-inch baking pan with cooking spray. Set aside.
3. Place all ingredients in a blender. Cover and blend on low speed about 30 seconds, or until smooth. Pour into greased baking pan.
4. Bake corn soufflé about 35 minutes, or until slightly brown. Let stand 5 minutes before serving.

Yield: 9 Servings

Cornmeal Patties
Arepas

Arepas are popular in Colombia and Venezuela. These patties are served as a side for breakfast, lunch, and dinner or as a snack on their own. Many think of them as a substitute for bread. You can find arepa flour (white cornmeal/harina de maíz blanca), in Latin markets or large supermarkets. This is how my Colombian aunt, Leyla Ali de Yacaman, makes hers.

1 cup white cornmeal
$^1/_4$ cup grated Parmesan cheese
1 teaspoon garlic powder
1 teaspoon salt
Dash of ground white pepper
1 $^1/_2$ cups milk, warmed
4 tablespoons unsalted butter, melted
Vegetable oil, for frying arepas
$^1/_2$ cup finely shredded mozzarella cheese

1. Combine cornmeal, Parmesan cheese, garlic powder, salt, and pepper in a medium bowl; mix well. Add milk and butter; mix well. Let stand 5 minutes.
2. Form dough into 8 patties (arepas), 3-inch in diameter by $^1/_2$-inch thick (see "tip"). Place on a wax paper-lined tray. Cover with plastic wrap and refrigerate 1 hour.
3. Pour oil into a large nonstick skillet to a depth of $^1/_4$-inch; heat over medium heat.
4. Fry arepas 2 to 3 minutes per side, or until golden brown. Drain on paper towels. Sprinkle each with 1 tablespoon mozzarella cheese. Serve immediately.

Yield: 8 Arepas

Tip:

✓ It is very important to wet your hands with water in between each patty you form. Not only will it add extra moisture to the dough (needed to prevent patty edges from cracking), but it will also prevent the dough from sticking to your hands.

Fried Sweet Plantains
Platanos Fritos/Maduros/Amarillos

Fried sweet plantains are extremely popular throughout the Caribbean and Latin America. We serve them the same way French fries are served in the United States. I think of them as sweet tropical French fries.

Vegetable oil, for frying plantains
2 ripe plantains (see "tip")

1. Pour oil into a medium skillet to a depth of $^1/_4$-inch; heat over medium heat.
2. Meanwhile, peel and slice plantains. Cut off both ends of each plantain, diagonally; score skin several times, lengthwise; peel skin away. Slice plantains diagonally into $^1/_2$-inch-thick slices.
3. Fry plantain slices about 2 minutes per side, or until golden brown. Drain on paper towels. Serve immediately.

Yield: 4 Servings

Tip:

✓ Ripe plantains have black skin. However, if you cannot find ripe plantains, buy green or semi-ripe plantains (plantains with a yellow skin and scattered black spots), and let them ripen at room temperature on your kitchen counter.

Green Bananas with Tomato Sauce
Guineos Verdes con Salsa de Tomate

A Honduran tropical favorite! Because green bananas ripen quickly, I advise you to prepare this dish as soon as you get them. This recipe comes from my family's long-time Honduran cook, Luz Hernandez.

4 green bananas, peeled (see "tip")
1 teaspoon salt
$^1/_2$ cup "Tomato Sauce" (see page 122), heated
Grated Parmesan cheese

1. Place bananas in a medium saucepan. Add salt and enough water to cover them by 1 inch; bring to a boil over medium heat. Reduce heat to low. Cook, turning occasionally, about 15 minutes, or until fork-tender. Drain well.
2. Arrange bananas on a medium platter. Top with tomato sauce. Sprinkle with cheese. Serve immediately.

Yield: 4 Bananas

Tip:

✓   See tip on page 24.

Grilled Corn
Maíz Asado

Grilling is my favorite way of cooking corn. The distinctive smoky flavor attained through grilling is unmatched by any other cooking method. I like to serve it as a side for grilled meats, pork, and poultry, or by itself as a snack.

4 ears yellow corn, husks and silky threads removed
4 tablespoons unsalted butter, melted
Salt and ground black pepper

1. Heat grill to medium heat.
2. Brush corn with butter. Sprinkle with salt and pepper.
3. Grill corn, turning occasionally, 18 to 20 minutes, or until some kernels turn dark golden brown. Serve immediately.

Yield: 4 Servings

Tips:
- ✓ For a smokier flavor, try grilling the corn a little longer until some kernels look burnt (black).
- ✓ Feeling adventurous? Spread grilled corn with mayonnaise, sprinkle with crumbled cotija cheese (queso seco) or grated Parmesan cheese, and drizzle with ketchup.

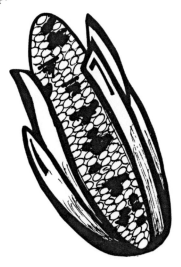

Grilled Green Onions
Cebollitas Asadas

Cebollitas asadas are a must-have with grilled meats. I like to serve them as an appetizer, too.

2 bunches green onions
Olive oil
Salt and ground black pepper
Lime wedges, for serving

1. Heat grill to medium heat.
2. Meanwhile, trim and season onions. Trim off root ends; rinse and pat dry; drizzle with oil. Sprinkle with salt and pepper.
3. Grill onions about $1^1/_2$ minutes per side, or until slightly charred. Serve with lime wedges immediately.

Yield: 4 Servings

Side Dishes/Acompañamientos

Pickled Onions
Encurtido de Cebolla

These fuchsia-colored onions are a traditional side to grilled meats throughout Central America. They will add an exceptional touch of color to just about any meal.

2 medium yellow onions, julienned
1 small beet, thinly sliced
1 jalapeño pepper, thinly sliced
1 bay leaf
2 cups warm water
1 $^1/_4$ cups distilled white vinegar
1 tablespoon salt
2 teaspoons sugar

1. Combine onion, beet, pepper, bay leaf, and water in a glass or plastic container with a tight-fitting lid. Set aside.
2. Combine vinegar, salt, and sugar in a small glass or plastic bowl; stir until salt and sugar dissolve. Pour over vegetables. Tightly close lid. Let pickle 3 days in refrigerator, shaking container twice a day, before serving.

Yield: About 4 Cups

Caution:

✓ Be careful when preparing and serving these onions, as the pickling solution stains.

Plantain Patties
Tortitas de Plátano

I like to think of these patties as plantain bread. This recipe comes from my family's cook, Luz. Serve them with a side of butter.

1 ripe plantain
2 tablespoons sugar
Pinch of ground cinnamon
2 tablespoons unsalted butter, melted
1 large egg
Plain bread crumbs (about 1 cup)
Vegetable oil, for frying patties

1. Cut off both ends of plantain; cut in half; leave skin on. Place plantain halves in a small saucepan. Add enough water to cover them by 1 inch; bring to a boil over medium heat. Cook 15 minutes. Drain well. Cool to the touch.

2. Peel plantain halves. Place in a food processor. Cover and process about 30 seconds, or until pureed. Transfer to a medium bowl. Add sugar, cinnamon, butter, and egg; mix well. Add bread crumbs; mix well. (Add more bread crumbs if the dough is too wet, and vice versa.) Let stand 5 minutes.

3. Form plantain mixture into 8 patties, 3-inch in diameter by $1/_4$-inch thick. Place on a wax paper-lined tray. Cover with plastic wrap and refrigerate 1 hour.

4. Pour oil into a medium nonstick skillet to a depth of $1/_4$-inch; heat over medium heat.

5. Fry patties about 2 minutes per side, or until golden brown. Drain on paper towels. Serve immediately.

Yield: 4 Servings

Red Beans and Rice
Gallo Pinto

Original to Nicaragua, this dish has crossed borders throughout Central America. "Gallo pinto" literally translates to "dappled rooster" in English. It was named this way due to the resemblance the combination of the white rice and the red beans has with a white rooster covered with reddish spots.

1 tablespoon olive oil
$^1/_2$ cup chopped yellow onion
$^1/_4$ cup chopped green bell pepper
$^1/_4$ cup chopped celery
$^1/_2$ teaspoon salt
Pinch of ground cayenne pepper
1 tablespoon store-bought minced garlic
1 cup long-grain white rice
1 (16-ounce) can red kidney beans, undrained
2 cups store-bought low-sodium chicken broth
1 bay leaf

1. Heat oil in a medium saucepan over medium heat. Add onion, bell pepper, celery, salt, and pepper; cook and stir about 5 minutes, or until vegetables are softened. Add garlic; cook and stir 30 seconds. Add rice; stir until rice grains look coated with oil. Add beans, broth, and bay leaf; mix well. Bring to a boil. Reduce heat to low. Cover and cook 17 to 20 minutes, or until most of the liquid is absorbed.
2. Remove saucepan from heat. Let stand, covered, 5 minutes. Fluff rice with a fork. Discard bay leaf. Serve immediately.

Yield: 4 to 6 Servings

Refried Beans
Frijoles Refritos

Refried beans are very popular in Mexico and Central America. The different ways to prepare them are many. My version calls for lots of chopped vegetables, which makes it chunky.

$^1/_4$ cup canola oil
1 cup chopped yellow onion
$^1/_2$ cup chopped green bell pepper
$^1/_2$ cup chopped celery
$^1/_2$ teaspoon ground cumin
$^1/_4$ teaspoon salt
$^1/_8$ teaspoon ground black pepper
1 (16-ounce) can refried beans

1. Heat oil in a medium skillet over medium heat. Add onion, bell pepper, celery, cumin, salt, and pepper; cook and stir about 5 minutes, or until vegetables are softened. Add beans; mix well. Cook, stirring continuously, about 3 minutes, or until thoroughly heated. Serve immediately.

Yield: About 2$^1/_2$ Cups

Rice with Corn
Arroz con Maíz

Corn's peak season is during summer months, thus making this dish an excellent accompaniment to add a summery touch to the table.

1 tablespoon canola oil
1 tablespoon store-bought minced garlic
$^1/_4$ teaspoon salt
$^1/_8$ teaspoon ground cayenne pepper
1 cup long-grain white rice
1 (15.25-ounce) can yellow whole kernel corn, drained
2 cups store-bought low-sodium chicken broth

1. Heat oil in a medium saucepan over medium heat. Add garlic, salt, and pepper; cook and stir 30 seconds. Add rice; stir until rice grains look coated with oil. Add corn and broth; mix well. Bring to a boil. Reduce heat to low. Cover and cook 15 to 17 minutes, or until most of the liquid is absorbed.
2. Remove saucepan from heat. Let stand, covered, 5 minutes. Fluff rice with a fork. Serve immediately.

Yield: 4 to 6 Servings

Rice with Pigeon Peas
Arroz con Gandules

A Puerto Rican staple! It's a traditional side during the Christmas holidays. This recipe comes from my sister-in-law Michelle.

1 tablespoon "Annatto Oil" (see page 117)
$^1/_2$ cup chopped yellow onion
$^1/_4$ cup chopped green bell pepper
$^1/_4$ cup chopped celery
4 slices bacon, cut into $^1/_2$-inch pieces
$^1/_2$ teaspoon salt
$^1/_4$ teaspoon ground coriander
$^1/_8$ teaspoon ground cayenne pepper
1 tablespoon store-bought minced garlic
1 cup long-grain white rice
1 (15-ounce) can green pigeon peas, undrained
2 cups store-bought low-sodium chicken broth
1 bay leaf

1. Heat oil in a medium saucepan over medium heat. Add onion, bell pepper, celery, bacon, salt, coriander, and pepper; cook and stir about 8 to 10 minutes, or until vegetables are softened and bacon starts to crisp. Add garlic; cook and stir 30 seconds. Add rice; stir until rice grains look coated with oil. Add peas, broth, and bay leaf; mix well. Bring to a boil. Reduce heat to low. Cover and cook 18 to 20 minutes, or until most of the liquid is absorbed.
2. Remove saucepan from heat. Let stand, covered, 5 minutes. Fluff rice with a fork. Discard bay leaf. Serve immediately.

Yield: 4 to 6 Servings

Rice with Vegetables
Arroz con Vegetales

I think of this side dish as two-in-one. I get both of my favorite sides—rice and vegetables—at once.

1 tablespoon canola oil
1 cup long-grain white rice
1 (10-ounce) can diced tomatoes with green chiles, drained
1(14.5-ounce) can mixed vegetables, drained
2 cups store-bought low-sodium chicken broth
$^1/_2$ teaspoon salt
$^1/_4$ teaspoon ground cumin
$^1/_4$ teaspoon yellow coloring powder (amarillo) (optional)
Pinch of ground cayenne pepper
Pinch of sugar

1. Heat oil in a medium saucepan over medium heat. Add rice; stir until rice grains look coated with oil. Add tomatoes, vegetables, broth, salt, cumin, coloring (if using), pepper, and sugar; mix well. Bring to a boil. Reduce heat to low. Cover and cook about 15 minutes, or until most of the liquid is absorbed.
2. Remove saucepan from heat. Let stand, covered, 5 minutes. Fluff rice with a fork. Serve immediately.

Yield: 4 to 6 Servings

Stuffed Mirlitons
Chancletas/Chayotes o Patastillos Rellenos

"Chancletas", which literally translates to "flip-flops" in English, are to Hondurans what twice-baked potatoes are to Americans. Why this name? I still can't figure it out myself. I guess they look like flip-flops to some. This recipe comes from my family's cook, Luz.

2 mirlitons
1 tablespoon olive oil
$^1/_2$ cup chopped yellow onion
$^1/_4$ cup chopped green bell pepper
$^1/_4$ cup chopped celery
$^1/_2$ teaspoon salt
$^1/_4$ teaspoon ground black pepper
$^1/_2$ cup "Honduran Cream" (see page 120)
4 tablespoons shredded Cheddar cheese

1. Place mirlitons in a medium saucepan. Add enough water to cover them by 2 inches; bring to a boil over medium heat. Cook about 1 hour, or until fork-tender. Drain well. Cool to the touch.
2. Cut mirlitons in half, lengthwise. Remove and discard seeds; scoop out pulp into a medium bowl. Set mirliton shells aside.
3. Mash mirliton pulp. Drain excess liquid. Set aside.
4. Heat oven to 350° F.
5. Heat oil in a medium skillet over medium heat. Add onion, bell pepper, celery, salt, and pepper; cook and stir about 5 minutes, or until vegetables are softened. Add reserved mashed mirliton pulp; mix well. Remove from heat. Add cream; mix well.
6. Stuff mirliton shells with mirliton mixture. Sprinkle each with 1 tablespoon cheese. Place on an ungreased baking sheet.
7. Bake stuffed mirlitons 5 minutes, or until cheese is melted. Let stand 5 minutes before serving.

Yield: 4 Servings

Twice-Fried Green Plantains
Tostones

Tostones are very popular throughout the Caribbean. Like with "Fried Sweet Plantains" (page 83), tostones are served the same way French fries are served in the United States. Many think of them as tropical French fries. "Cuban Garlic Sauce" (page 119) makes an excellent dipping sauce for them.

Vegetable oil, for frying plantains
2 green plantains
Salt and ground cayenne pepper

1. Pour oil into a large skillet to a depth of 1-inch; heat over medium heat.
2. Meanwhile, peel and slice plantains. Cut off both ends of each plantain, cross-wise; score skin several times, lengthwise; peel skin away. Slice plantains crosswise into 1-inch-thick slices.
3. Fry plantain slices about 2 minutes, or until light gold. Drain on paper towels. Cool to the touch.
4. Place 1 plantain slice on a work surface. Flatten it with the back of a large spatula into a $^1/_4$-inch-thick slice. Repeat with remaining plantain slices.
5. Fry flattened plantain slices about 1 minute per side, or until golden brown. Drain on paper towels. Sprinkle with salt and pepper. Serve immediately.

Yield: 4 Servings

Tip:

✓ For crispier tostones, fry plantain slices for a longer time on step 5.

White Rice
Arroz Blanco

This versatile rice couldn't be easier and quicker to make. It's an excellent choice when time is limited.

1 tablespoon canola oil
1 cup long-grain white rice
$1/_2$ teaspoon salt
2 cups water

1. Heat oil in a medium saucepan over medium heat. Add rice and salt; stir until rice grains look coated with oil. Add water; mix well. Bring to a boil. Reduce heat to low. Cover and cook about 15 minutes, or until most of the liquid is absorbed.
2. Remove saucepan from heat. Let stand, covered, 5 minutes. Fluff rice with a fork. Serve immediately.

Yield: 4 Servings

Yellow Rice
Arroz Amarillo

Yellow coloring powder (amarillo) is the powder used to give this rice its bright yellow color. However, if you are unable to find it, do not stress. The "Annatto Oil" (page 117) in it will still give it a yellow color too, but much lighter. Serve it as a side to add a touch of color to meals.

1 tablespoon "Annatto Oil" (see page 117)
1 cup long-grain white rice
$^1/_2$ teaspoon salt
2 cups store-bought low-sodium chicken broth
$^1/_4$ teaspoon yellow coloring powder (amarillo)

1. Heat oil in a medium saucepan over medium heat. Add rice and salt; stir until rice grains look coated with oil. Add broth and coloring; mix well. Bring to a boil. Reduce heat to low. Cover and cook about 15 minutes, or until most of the liquid is absorbed.
2. Remove saucepan from heat. Let stand, covered, 5 minutes. Fluff rice with a fork. Serve immediately.

Yield: 4 Servings

Yucca with Cuban Garlic Sauce
Yuca con Mojo de Ajo

This is the Cuban way of preparing yucca. Traditionally, it has been served as a side dish for meat, pork, or poultry. I think it makes a great snack on its own too.

2 pounds yucca, peeled and cut crosswise into 3- to 4-inch pieces
1 tablespoon salt
$^1/_2$ cup "Cuban Garlic Sauce" (see page 119), heated

1. Place yucca in a large saucepan. Add salt and enough water to cover it by 1 inch; bring to a boil over high heat. Reduce heat to medium. Cook 15 to 18 minutes, or until fork-tender. Drain well. Cool to the touch.
2. Cut yucca pieces in half, lengthwise; remove and discard stringy fibers from the center.
3. Arrange yucca on a large platter. Top with garlic sauce. Serve immediately.

Yield: 4 Servings

Yucca with Tomato Sauce
Yuca con Salsa de Tomate

The previous recipe describes the Cuban style of serving boiled yucca, whereas this one describes the Honduran style. Serve them interchangeably.

2 pounds yucca, peeled and cut crosswise into 3- to 4-inch pieces
1 tablespoon salt
$^1/_2$ cup "Tomato Sauce" (see page 122), heated
Grated Parmesan cheese

1. Place yucca in a large saucepan. Add salt and enough water to cover it by 1 inch; bring to a boil over high heat. Reduce heat to medium. Cook 15 to 18 minutes, or until fork-tender. Drain well. Cool to the touch.
2. Cut yucca pieces in half, lengthwise; remove and discard stringy fibers from the center.
3. Arrange yucca on a large platter. Top with tomato sauce. Sprinkle with cheese. Serve immediately.

Yield: 4 Servings

Desserts
Postres

Desserts/Postres

Candied Acorn Squash
Ayote en Dulce

A Honduran favorite! Piloncillo, also known as atado, panela, or raspadura, is unrefined brown sugar cane molded into a cone or a square. It can be found in Latin markets or large supermarkets. Traditionally, candied acorn squash has been served as a dessert only; however, I like to serve it as a side dish too.

1 pound piloncillo or 4 cups firmly packed light brown sugar
4 cups water
1 acorn squash (about 1³/₄ pounds), peeled, halved, seeded, and cut into 1-inch cubes

1. Combine piloncillo (or sugar) and water in a medium saucepan. Bring to a boil over medium heat. Cook, stirring occasionally, 20 minutes, or until piloncillo dissolves and liquid is slightly thicker. Add squash; cook, turning occasionally, 30 minutes or until fork-tender. Serve warm.

Yield: 4 Servings

103

Corn Cake
Pastel de Maíz

On my last trip to Mexico City, I had the chance to try this cake. It was simply delicious! As strange as it may sound, corn gives this cake an exotic and delectable taste. Using a cake mix and canned corn makes this cake easy to prepare.

1 (18.25-ounce) box yellow cake mix
1 (14.75-ounce) can cream-style sweet corn
$^1/_3$ cup canola oil
3 large eggs
Pinch of salt
Powdered sugar, for garnish

1. Heat oven to 350° F.
2. Grease a 10-inch baking tube pan with cooking spray. Set aside.
3. Combine cake mix, corn, oil, eggs, and salt in a large mixing bowl. Beat on low speed about 30 seconds. Stop mixer; scrape bowl sides. Beat on medium speed 3 minutes. Pour into greased baking pan.
4. Bake cake about 40 minutes, or until a toothpick inserted in center comes out clean.
5. Remove baking pan from oven. Cool to the touch.
6. Invert cake onto a serving platter. Let cool.
7. To serve, sift sugar on top. (see "tip")

Yield: 8 to 16 Servings

Tip:

✓ It is very important to wait until the cake is completely cool to sift the powdered sugar on it; otherwise, it will be absorbed.

Dulce de Leche Cookie Sandwiches
Alfajores

Dulce de leche, also known as cajeta in México, arequipe in Colombia, manjar in Chile, and caramelized milk in the United States, is believed to have originated in Argentina. It is one of the most popular and beloved sweets throughout Latin America. These days, you can find bottled or canned dulce de leche (cajeta) in Latin markets or large supermarkets. Alfajores are very popular cookies throughout South America. Using store-bought cookies and dulce de leche (cajeta) makes this version easy, fast, and versatile.

24 store-bought vanilla wafer cookies, divided
3 teaspoons store-bought dulce de leche (cajeta)
Powdered sugar

1. Spoon $^1/_4$ teaspoon dulce de leche on center of flat side of 12 of the cookies. Press remaining 12 cookies, flat side down, on top. Sift sugar on top. Serve immediately.

Yield: 12 Alfajores

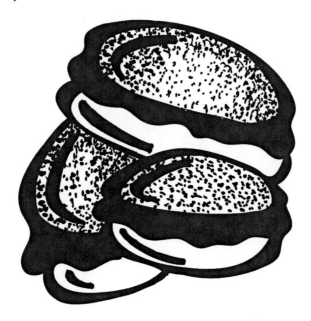

Dulce de Leche Crepes
Crepas con Dulce de Leche

This particular dessert couldn't get any easier and quicker with store-bought dulce de leche (cajeta) and crepes.

1 (8-ounce) package cream cheese, softened
$^1/_2$ cup store-bought dulce de leche (cajeta)
1 (10-count, 9-inch) bag store-bought crepes, heated

1. Beat cheese and dulce de leche with an electric mixer in a medium bowl on low speed until smooth.
2. Spread 2 heaping tablespoons cheese mixture on each crepe. (see "tip") Fold in half to form a half-moon; fold in half again to form a triangle. Set aside. Repeat with remaining crepes.
3. To serve, drizzle crepes with dulce de leche, if desired.

Yield: 5 to 10 Servings

Tip:
 ✓ If cream cheese mixture is too firm to spread over crepes easily, soften it in a microwave-safe dish on high at 15 second intervals until desired consistency is achieved.

Flan

Flan is to Spaniards what crème caramel is to French or what crema caramella is to Italians. This Spanish custard has become a classic favorite throughout the Caribbean and Latin America. Nowadays, you can enjoy a variety of flavors, from chocolate or coffee to dulce de leche flans, to name a few. I like to stick to the classic flan. This is how my sister-in-law Michelle taught me to make it.

Caramel: (see "caution")
$^1/_2$ cup sugar

Flan:
1 cup milk
1 (14-ounce) can sweetened condensed milk
2 large eggs
1 teaspoon vanilla extract
Pinch of salt

1. Heat oven to 350° F.
2. Make caramel. Cook sugar in a small skillet over medium-low heat, without stirring, but carefully swirling skillet, about 12 minutes, or until it evenly melts and turns amber in color. Carefully pour 1 tablespoon caramel into six (6-ounce) ramekins. Place ramekins in a baking pan.
3. Place milk, condensed milk, eggs, vanilla, and salt in a blender. Cover and blend on low speed about 30 seconds, or until smooth. Strain into ramekins.
4. Pour enough hot water into baking pan to come halfway up exterior sides of ramekins.
5. Bake flans about 45 minutes, or until a knife inserted in center comes out clean.
6. Remove baking pan from oven. Place ramekins on wire rack. Let cool. Refrigerate about 2 hours, or until thoroughly chilled.

Yield: 6 Flans

Caution:
   ✓ You need to be extremely careful when making and pouring the caramel, as it will burn you if it gets on you.

Peruvian Custard
Suspiro Limeño

I think of suspiro limeño as the stove-top Peruvian version of "Flan" (page 107).

1 (14-ounce) can sweetened condensed milk
1 (12-ounce) can evaporated milk
$^1/_2$ cup milk
4 egg yolks, slightly beaten
Pinch of salt
1 teaspoon vanilla extract
Store-bought sweetened whipped cream, for serving
Ground cinnamon, for sprinkling

1. Combine condensed milk, evaporated milk, milk, egg yolks, and salt in a small saucepan; stir well. Cook over medium heat, stirring continuously, about 10 minutes, or until slightly thicker. Remove from heat. Add vanilla; stir well.
2. Divide custard evenly among 6 individual dessert cups. Let cool. Refrigerate about 2 hours, or until set.
3. To serve, generously top with whipped cream and sprinkle with cinnamon.

Yield: 6 Servings

Pineapple Jam
Mermelada de Piña

This tropical jam makes a great filler in "Pineapple Turnovers" (page 110), as well as in cakes or as a topper on ice cream.

1 (1-pound, 4-ounce) can crushed pineapple in pineapple juice, undrained
1 tablespoon cornstarch
$^3/_4$ cup sugar, or to taste
Pinch of salt
1 tablespoon unsalted butter

1. Drain pineapple, reserving $^1/_4$ cup juice.
2. Whisk cornstarch into reserved $^1/_4$ cup pineapple juice in a small glass bowl until smooth. Set aside.
3. Combine pineapple, sugar, and salt in a small non-reactive saucepan; mix well. Cook over medium heat, stirring frequently, 15 to 18 minutes, or until most of the liquid evaporates.
4. Stir cornstarch mixture. Pour over pineapple mixture. Cook, stirring continuously, about 3 minutes, or until slightly thicker. Remove from heat. Add butter; stir until melted. Serve warm or chilled. Store in a glass or plastic container in refrigerator.

Yield: About 1$^1/_2$ Cups

Pineapple Turnovers
Empanadas de Piña

The recipe for these yummy treats comes from my mother, Jeanette. Serve them to add a tropical ending to meals.

Dough (Masa):
2 cups all-purpose flour
$^1/_4$ teaspoon salt
1 (8-ounce) package cream cheese, softened and cut into small pieces
$^1/_2$ cup (1 stick) cold unsalted butter, cut into small pieces

Filling (Relleno):
$1^1/_2$ cups "Pineapple Jam" (see page 109), cooled

1. Sift flour and salt into a medium bowl.
2. Place flour mixture, cheese, and butter in a food processor. Cover and pulse until dough starts to come together into a ball.
3. Remove dough from bowl and shape into a ball. Wrap with plastic wrap and refrigerate 30 minutes.
4. Heat oven to 375° F.
5. Roll out half of the dough on a floured work surface to $^1/_8$-inch thickness. (Keep remaining dough in refrigerator.) Cut dough into circles with a 4-inch cutter. Spoon 1 tablespoon jam on center of each dough circle. Brush edges with water. Fold in half to form a half-moon. Seal edges by crimping with a fork. Place empanadas on an ungreased baking sheet. Repeat with remaining dough.
6. Coat empanada tops with cooking spray.
7. Bake empanadas about 20 minutes, or until light golden brown. Let stand 5 minutes before serving.

Yield: About 2 Dozen

Rice Pudding
Arroz con Leche

Rice pudding, like "Flan" (page 107), is original to Spain and is a classical favorite throughout Latin America. The different recipes are countless. This particular version comes from my family's cook, Luz.

1 cup medium-grain white rice
2 cups water
1 cinnamon stick
Pinch of salt
4 cups milk
$^1/_2$ cup sugar
1 (1.5-ounce) box raisins
1 teaspoon vanilla extract
Ground cinnamon, for sprinkling

1. Combine rice, water, cinnamon stick, and salt in a medium nonstick saucepan; mix well. Bring to a boil over medium heat. Reduce heat to low. Cover and cook 15 minutes.
2. Add milk and sugar; cook, stirring frequently, 45 minutes. Add raisins; cook, stirring frequently, 5 to 10 minutes, or until slightly thicker. Remove saucepan from heat. Add vanilla; stir well. Discard cinnamon stick.
3. Divide pudding evenly among 6 to 8 individual dessert cups. Sprinkle with cinnamon. Serve warm or chilled.

Yield: 6 to 8 Servings

Strawberries in Condensed Milk
Fresas en Leche Condensada

Condensed milk is very popular in Latin America. We use it to make desserts (such as dulce de leche, "Flan" (page 107), and "Three-Milks Cake" (page 113), among others), drinks, or just to sip on. As I was growing up, I remember my mother, Jeanette, packing my lunch box every school day with a miniature (3.5-ounce) can of sweetened condensed milk, which I would sip on through class. Those were the days! This easy and fast-to-prepare recipe comes from her. It makes a yummy treat by itself or as a topping on cakes or ice cream.

1 pound fresh strawberries, quartered
1 (14-ounce) can sweetened condensed milk

1. Combine strawberries and condensed milk in a large bowl; mix well. Cover and refrigerate 2 hours; stir before serving.

Yield: 4 Servings

Three-Milks Cake
Tres Leches

This super-moist cake originated in Nicaragua and has managed to cross borders throughout the Caribbean and Latin America. It is literally soaked in three different milks. Traditionally, these milks are evaporated, condensed, and whole milk; however, I prefer to use heavy cream in place of whole milk for a creamier texture. The number of recipes for this cake is countless. My version uses a cake mix to make it easier and quicker to prepare.

Cake:
1 (18.25-ounce) box white cake mix, plus ingredients to prepare cake

Milk Syrup:
1 (12-ounce) can evaporated milk
1 (14-ounce) can sweetened condensed milk
2 cups heavy whipping cream

Frosting:
1 (8-ounce) tub frozen whipped topping, thawed in refrigerator

1. Prepare cake mix as directed on package, using a13x9x2-inch baking pan. (see "tip")
2. About 3 minutes before cake is done, prepare milk syrup. Place evaporated milk, condensed milk, and heavy cream in a blender. Cover and blend on low speed about 30 seconds, or until well blended.
3. Remove baking pan from oven. Slowly pour milk syrup over warm cake. Let cool. Cover and refrigerate about 4 hours or until thoroughly chilled.
4. Frost cake top with whipped topping. Cut into 12 individual slices. Garnish each with 1 maraschino cherry, if desired. Serve immediately. Store in refrigerator.

Yield: 12 Servings

Tip:
✓ Some white cake mixes offer both an egg-white and a whole-egg recipe to prepare cake mix. Follow the egg-white recipe.

Variation:

✓ To add a coconut flavor to this cake, substitute one 13.5-ounce can coconut milk for the can of evaporated milk.

✓ To add a coffee flavor to this cake, use $1\frac{1}{2}$ cups heavy whipping cream instead of 2 cups, and add $\frac{1}{2}$ cup coffee liqueur to the milk syrup.

Basics

Básicos

Basics/Básicos

Annatto Oil
Aceite de Achiote

Annatto seeds give annatto oil its orange-reddish color and earthy flavor. They can be found in Latin markets or large supermarkets.

1 cup canola oil or olive oil
$^1/_4$ cup annatto seeds

1. Heat oil in a small skillet over medium heat. Add annatto seeds; cook and stir about 3 minutes, or until oil turns orange-red in color.
2. Remove skillet from heat. Let cool.
3. Strain annatto oil into an airtight container. Discard annatto seeds. Cover and store in refrigerator.

Yield: 1 Cup

Caution:

✓ Be careful when cooking with this oil, as it stains.

Chimichurri

Thank Argentineans for this pesto-like sauce. Chimichurri is to Argentineans what "Mojo de Ajo" (page 119) is to Cubans or what pesto is to Italians. Traditionally, it has been made with parsley; however, for a variation, many cooks use a combination of parsley and cilantro or cilantro by itself. I like to use both. Use it to marinate and top meats, pork, or poultry.

1 bunch cilantro, finely chopped
1 bunch parsley, finely chopped
2 tablespoons store-bought minced garlic
1 cup olive oil
$^1/_4$ cup lime juice
1 teaspoon salt
$^1/_8$ teaspoon ground black pepper

1. Combine all ingredients in a medium glass or plastic bowl; mix well. Cover and refrigerate 2 hours before serving.

Yield: About 2 Cups

Cuban Garlic Sauce
Mojo de Ajo

Traditionally, it has been served as a dipping sauce for "Tostones" (page 95) or as a topper for "Yuca con Mojo de Ajo" (page 98) or "Roasted Pork" (page 65). I like to use it to top grilled fish, meats, pork, or poultry too.

$^1/_2$ cup olive oil
2 tablespoons store-bought minced garlic
$^1/_4$ teaspoon salt
$^1/_8$ teaspoon ground cumin
Pinch of ground cayenne pepper
2 tablespoons lime juice

1. Heat oil in a small non-reactive saucepan over medium heat. Add garlic, salt, cumin, and pepper; cook, stirring continuously, 1 minute. Add lime juice; stir well.
2. Transfer sauce to a small glass or plastic bowl. Serve immediately.

Yield: About $^2/_3$ Cup

Honduran Cream
Mantequilla

Hondurans use mantequilla the same way Americans use sour cream. It makes an excellent topper on "Fried Sweet Plantains" (page 83) or filler in "Baleadas" (page 41).

1 (8-ounce) container sour cream
1 tablespoon milk
$^1/_4$ teaspoon salt

1. Combine all ingredients in a small bowl; mix well. Cover and refrigerate 1 hour; stir before serving.

Yield: About 1 Cup

Jalapeño Sauce
Salsa Jalapeña

This sauce is especially for those who enjoy extremely pepper-hot foods. Traditionally, it is served on grilled meats. However, I like to serve it on pork, poultry, and seafood too.

1 tablespoon olive oil
1 large yellow onion, julienned
$^1/_2$ teaspoon salt
$^1/_2$ teaspoon sugar
2 tablespoons masa harina
1 (7-ounce) can pickled sliced jalapeño peppers, drained
2 cups heavy whipping cream

1. Heat oil in a medium non-reactive saucepan over medium heat. Add onion, salt, and sugar; cook and stir about 5 minutes, or until onion is softened. Add masa harina; cook, stirring continuously, 1 minute. Add peppers and heavy cream; mix well. Cook, stirring continuously, 3 to 5 minutes, or until slightly thicker.
2. Transfer sauce to a medium glass or plastic bowl. Serve immediately.

Yield: About 2 Cups

Tomato Sauce
Salsa de Tomate

Cilantro adds an exceptionally refreshing taste to this sauce. It is often used to top "Honduran-Style Enchiladas" (page 54), "Plantain Chips with Ground Beef" (page 59), and "Yucca with Pork Cracklings" (page 72). Use it as a ketchup substitute too.

1 tablespoon canola oil
1 (8-ounce) can tomato sauce
$^1/_4$ cup cilantro leaves
Pinch of ground cayenne pepper
Pinch of sugar

1. Heat oil in a small non reactive skillet over medium-low heat.
2. Place tomato sauce, cilantro, pepper, and sugar in a blender. Cover and blend on low speed about 1 minute, or until smooth. Pour into skillet. Cook and stir about 5 minutes, or until oil and sauce are thoroughly combined and heated.
3. Transfer sauce to a small glass or plastic bowl. Serve immediately.

Yield: About $^1/_2$ Cup

Index

At last, Latin favorites simplified. *Shortcuts to 100 Best Latin Recipes* shares creative and time-saving ideas on how to combine convenience foods with fresh ingredients to prepare no-fail, homemade-tasting, all-time favorite Latino recipes that are simply delicious. Explore from piña coladas, empanadas, guacamole, salsas, tortilla soup, churrasco with chimichurri, feijoada, cuban sandwiches, fried sweet plantains, dulce de leche, to tres leches, to name a few. Buen provecho!

About the Author

Sergio Yibrin was born in San Pedro Sula, Honduras, and now lives in New Orleans, Louisiana (a city whose diverse and rich culture highly contributes to its delectable and unique Cajun and Creole cuisine, making it a world-class culinary destination). He was educated at Loyola University New Orleans and graduated with a Bachelor of Business Administration in 1998 and a Master of Business Administration in 2002. Sergio is a self-taught cook whose passion is to entertain family and friends cooking simple, yet delicious Latin meals. www.sergioyibrin.com

978-0-595-46827-0
0-595-46827-6

Printed in the United States
133291LV00004B/13-54/A

9 780595 468270